HOUSE ARREST and CORRECTIONAL POLICY
POLICY
Doing Time at Home

STUDIES IN CRIME, LAW AND JUSTICE

Series Editor: James A. Inciardi,
Division of Criminal Justice, University of Delaware

Studies in Crime, Law and Justice contains original research formulations and new analytic perspectives on continuing important issues of crime and the criminal justice and legal systems. Volumes are research based but are written in nontechnical language to allow for use in courses in criminal justice, criminology, law, social problems, and related subjects.

Studies are both contributions to the research literature and ideal text supplements, and are of interest to academics, professionals, and students.

HOUSE ARREST
and CORRECTIONAL POLICY
Doing Time at Home

BY
Richard A. Ball
C. Ronald Huff
J. Robert Lilly

STUDIES IN CRIME, LAW AND JUSTICE ■ Volume 3

SAGE PUBLICATIONS
The Publishers of Professional Social Science
Newbury Park   Beverly Hills   London   New Delhi

For information address:

SAGE Publications, Inc.
2111 West Hillcrest Drive
Newbury Park, California 91320

SAGE Publications Inc.   SAGE Publications Ltd.
275 South Beverly Drive   28 Banner Street
Beverly Hills   London EC1Y 8QE
California 90212   England

SAGE PUBLICATIONS India Pvt. Ltd.
M-32 Market
Greater Kailash I
New Delhi 110 048 India

Printed in the United States of America

Library of Congress Cataloging-in-Publication Data

Ball, Richard A., 1936-
    House arrest and correctional policy : doing time at home /
  Richard A. Ball, C. Ronald Huff, J. Robert Lilly.
      p.   cm— (Studies in crime, law, and justice ; v. 3)
  Bibliography: p.
  ISBN 0-8039-2969-2   ISBN 0-8039-2970-6 (pbk.)
  1. Home detention—United States. 2. Prisoners—
Deinstitutionalization—United States. 3. Juvenile delinquents—
Deinstitutionalization—United States. 4. Criminal justice,
Administration of—United States. 5. Juvenile justice,
Administration of—United States. I. Huff, C. Ronald. II. Lilly,
J. Robert. III. Title. IV. Series.
HV9469.B18 1987
364.6'8—dc19   87-28349
                                        CIP

Contents

Foreword

There is something disquieting about the use of house arrest as a procedure for dealing with alleged criminal offenders before trial or convicted criminals after trial. The discomfort is increased when house arrest is accompanied by the use of electronic monitoring devices that signal a person's whereabouts to a central monitoring station. The authors of the present volume share this sense of unease, and they are meticulous in setting out both the disadvantages and the merits of house arrest and its accompanying tactics.

On the face of it, opposition to the increasing use of house arrest may seem based more on hazy romantic notions than on substantial grounds. There is no question, assuredly, that the employment of house arrest can save significant amounts of money, an obvious benefit, especially if the result is achieved in a more benign manner than that associated with usual methods. At the same time, persons who are allowed to serve correctional time in their own houses, perhaps being permitted to leave the premises for work or on errands, almost uniformly elect to undergo this punishment rather than incarceration in a jail or prison. Their preference, however, need not be determinative of the issue: Rapists often will voluntarily elect to undergo castration rather than serve time, and some thieves might well prefer the mutilation of a clipped ear or a severed hand to 10 years in a state prison. Self-determination under pressure probably cannot be regarded as the definitive criterion for endorsement or rejection of social policy.

On what foundations, then, do criticisms of house arrest lie? The authors point out that traditional use of the procedure in European and South American nations against political prisoners has created an uneasiness about house arrest. The fear of invasion of our lives by technology and the shrinking of the inviolate territorial reach of our privacy also seem to play a significant role in opposition to house arrest. Neither of these concerns, however, appears to be notably substantial when measured against the awful deprivations of imprisonment, the usual alternative to house arrest. The feeling that house arrest might come to be employed against persons who otherwise would not be enmeshed in the criminal justice system, however, also undoubtedly contributes to concern about its growing use.

The idea that a man's and a woman's house is their castle—their sanctuary, not their prison—seems to lie particularly close to the heart of concerns about house arrest. The concept of the home as a castle has a long and intriguing history in Anglo-Saxon jurisprudence. Its first major enunciation is in Title 4 of the second book of the *Digest* (or *Pandects*) of Justinian: "*Domus Tutissimum cuique refugium atque receptaculum*" (Watson, 1985: I, 45-46). The *Digest*, part of what later became known as the *Corpus Juris Civilis* (which also included the *Code*, the *Institutes*, and the *Novels*), represented a monumental codification of past and present Roman jurisprudence, the greatest contribution of Justinian's long reign (Gibbon, 1776: chap. 44). The *Digest* was completed in 533 A.D. It is a comprehensive anthology of the ancient legal writers and largely represents the stunning scholarship of Tribonian, Justinian's *quaestor*, or minister of legislation and propaganda. Tribonian was an anomaly, a man possessed of a profound learning in the law and its history and of juridical wisdom unsurpassed in his time and rarely in ours (Honore, 1978), yet also a man notoriously corrupt and dishonest.

The snippet in the *Digest* relating to a man's house refers to restrictions on the power of the state to summon persons before courts (*De in Jus Vocando*). You could not interrupt services for the dead, or interfere with a judge hearing a case, or take a bride away from her marriage ceremony in response to a court order to appear. This doctrine was traced back to Gaius, a second-century jurist, who in his commentary on Table I of the Twelve Tables (c. 450 B.C.) was said (for Tribonian's assignment encouraged updating and editing, and the originals often are no longer available) to have written: "Most thought that no one can be summoned from his house because this is an individual's safest refuge and shelter and one who summons him from there is held to exercise force" (Watson, 1985: I, 46). (Another translator renders the key phrase of the rule as follows: "The house of every individual should be for him a perfectly secure refuge and shelter"; Scott, 1932: II, 275). Gaius specified that it was permissible, however, to summon a person standing at the door of his house, partaking of the baths, or attending the theater. Further gloss on the doctrine had been supplied by Paulus a century and a half later in the first book of his edictal commentary, where he was said to have taken a more limited view of the sanctity of the home: "Although one who is at home can at times be summoned, yet no one ought to be dragged from his home."

In essence, then, the Justinian code, which came to form the basis not only of Anglo-Saxon law but that of numerous continental countries, declared that a person's home provided a limited protection, not far different from that allowed today against process servers, though even this shelter has been eroded by "constructive service" procedures, which allow a summons to be left on the threshold of a person known to be inside.

In 1581, William Lambard indicated the survival of the Justinian code position for more than 13 centuries when he noted in *Eirenarcha*, his handbook for England's lay justices of the peace, that "a man's house is his castle, which he may defend with force against any private army that shall invade him" (Book I, Chap. 18). Sir Edward Coke gave the theme further vigor 23 years later, in *Semayne's Case* (1604). Peter Semayne and George Berisford had been tenants in a London house. Berisford died, leaving "diverse goods" to Richard Gresham. Gresham, armed with a writ, and in company of the sheriff and his aides, was blocked by Semayne from entering the house to get his property, though the door at first was open. Lord Coke, ruling for Semayne, went back to Justinian: "The house of every one is to him as his castle and fortress, as well as for defense against injury and violence, as for his repose" (p. 91).

Coke later would reiterate this theme in Chapter 73 of the Third Institute, published in 1644, and thereby firmly establish the basis for recurrent reference to the axim as epitomizing English sensitivity to protection and privacy within the home. A reading of *Semayne's Case*, however, hardly allows so heady a conclusion. Most of the case is taken up with setting out conditions under which the authorities are allowed to breach the door of a residence. "The house of any one is not a castle or privilege but for himself," Coke declared, among other things, and "shall not extend to protect any person who flieth to his house to prevent a lawful execution" (p. 93). What went wrong for the sheriff's forces in dealing with Peter Semayne was only that when he had shut that door in their faces, "that which he may well do by law" (p. 93), the authorities had failed to make a proper request to have it reopened. Had they done so they would have been well within the bounds of their common-law rights to gain entry. (See Hale, 1736/1773: II, 202).

The Justinian doctrine, nonetheless, had at least one important implication in early English law. To set fire to the humblest cottage was decreed a heinous felony, though to set fire to a unique picture or a priceless tapestry was no crime at all (Turner, 1966: 249).

Later writers, both legal and literary, picked from such bare bones what viewpoint they sought to advance. Those with legal training hardly took the idea of the integrity of the home as anything more serious than a pious metaphor; those with humanistic instincts tended to make more of the idea; while realists portrayed it for what it truly was, a cliché seen by law persons as a bulwark, but in fact one with soft, insubstantial footings.

There clearly was something inherent in the Justinian code pronouncement that appealed to people's values and sentiments. In the literary realm, John Dryden in his first comedy, *The Wild Gallant* (1669: Act I, Scene II) had Loveby, a man given to bombastic statement, chide his landlady for driving him from his residence by her scolding: "My lodging, as long as I rent it, is my castle," he says. The landlady berates him about his debts to her. Feeling unjustly discredited because of, in the original language, "a lowsy, Paltry summ of Money," Loveby tells her that none should scold in their own cause, since this is what lawyers are paid for. Quite understandably, neither Samuel Pepys nor King Charles thought much of Dryden's play when they saw it in London a few weeks after the opening ("ill acted and . . . so poor a thing as I never saw in my life almost," Pepys wrote in his diary; Latham and Matthews, 1971: IV, 56).

Later, Ralph Waldo Emerson in the essay "Wealth" in *English Traits* (1856: 167) wrote rather caustically that "whatever surely sweetness possession can give, is tested in England to the dregs." He noted in this context that in England "the house is a castle which the King cannot enter." The reference was not altogether flattering since class consciousness in England was viewed with disfavor by Emerson. "There is no country," he wrote, "in which so absolute a homage is paid to wealth" (p. 157).

It was Charles Dickens, though, who set the proper tone for the ancient Justinian doctrine. In *Dombey and Son*, Mrs. MacStinger, a domineering landlady, ineffectually tries to keep out a young visitor to her boarder by inquiring "whether an Englishman's house was his castle or not" (Dickens, 1848: chap. 9). In *Great Expectations,* Joe Gargery, the unsophisticated blacksmith, "a mild, good-natured, sweet-tempered, easygoing, foolish, dear fellow," deplores a local burglary by observing that "a Englishman's house is his Castle, and castles must not be busted 'cept when done in war time" (Dickens, 1861: chap. 57). These sentiments, that a house is like unto a castle, as conveyed by Dickens seem almost like class yearnings—that I'm as good as you—as well as maudlin aspirations of the underdogs to be treated in the same manner as the gentry.

In all, the shards gleaned from the early Roman juris-consuls have shown considerable vitality. There is something attractive, something devoutly to be desired, resting within the doctrine that there exists some place of tranquility, some sanctum, that ought not be penetrated by any force or any person without invitation. Perhaps it is this ill-defined but powerful feeling that lies at the core of appraisal of the house arrest movement. Certainly the doctrine of the inviolability of a person's domicile carried the day in 1925 in Detroit when Clarence Darrow successfully relied on it to defend Ossian Sweet, a black physician, who had shot to death a member of a mob of people outside his house, seemingly threatening his family because it had crossed the color line by moving into an all-white neighborhood (Weinberg, 1971).

All told, a decent test of house arrest might well be to ask yourself: If I were convicted of, say, drunk driving, would I prefer a $200 fine and 30 days in jail to, say, 90 days of mandatory confinement to my house after work and on weekends and a $400 charge? If the latter, would my preference for home confinement continue if I had an electronic bracelet attached to my ankle or a monitor wrapped around my waist so that the authorities could make certain that I was where I was supposed to be when I was supposed to be there? And what would be my views if different parts of the hypothetical were altered, such as the nature of the offense, the ratio of jail time (or probation time) to the length of house arrest, the monetary charges attached to the diverse dispositions, the amount of time that must be spent within the house, and the intensity of the monitoring? The variables of significance and the range of options within them run to a formidable length. Individual personality differences, for instance, undoubtedly will influence an assessment of house arrest. Gustave de Beaumont and Alexis de Tocqueville (1833/1964: 121), examining America's experiment with the "silent system" of incarceration at Philadelphia and at Auburn, New York, in the nineteenth century, remarked wryly that deprivation of conversation might be all right for Americans, "whose character is taciturn and reflective," but would be an unholy cruelty to the gregarious French. Similarly, house confinement can be something of a pleasure, or at worst a minor irritant, to a Wall Street swindler, whose residence is supplied with a spouse as well as an indoor swimming pool and other cozy amenities, and whose business can be carried on by telephone. To a teenage burglar, banned from the Saturday night dance, cut off from street associations with friends, and thrown into constant association with stern and disapproving parents in a small ghetto apartment, house arrest takes on a very different dimension. Note, in this connection, the sentence in 1985 (though still under appeal) of a man in Los Angeles to 30 days of house arrest in one of the tenement apartments he was accused of allowing to exist in wretched condition. But note too that the offender, a 61-year-old neurosurgeon, was specifically allowed by the judge to take with him clean sheets, reading material, a television, and a private security guard.

Fair assessment of house arrest is a complicated matter if the aim is to provide empirical evaluation of the policy in regard to cost, reduction of recidivism, impact upon offenders, and the response of the population in general and the criminal justice system in particular. Absent adequate experimental designs—things such as immutable guidelines and random assignments—numerical statements of impact, as Professors Ball, Huff, and Lilly clearly point out, are not as yet possible. There is, however, a wealth of important information in this book about how particular programs appear to be working, their successes and their problems.

The authors also direct a large part of their discussion to a comprehensive review of contemporary legal doctrines—particularly those relating to privacy—that might come to play a part in this emergent correctional approach. They point out that house arrest has surfaced in a period of conservative politics, in which the spirit of the times is coldly hostile to the criminal offender. Tough punitive policies, though, demand new jails and prisons, and the mood of the citizenry, while unsympathetic to lower-class law violators, is preeminently fiscally self-interested, no more willing to be taxed for prison construction than for food stamp and other welfare programs. House arrest appeals to the cost-conscious. An advocate, quoted in this monograph, observes with a grandiloquent tone that implies that the whole matter is reducible to a single element: "This concept that is beginning to sweep the nation, beyond all doubt, is the greatest thing to happen to the American taxpayer in memory." Readers will find the authors of the book a good deal more restrained, more thorough and wary, less doctrinaire.

It is one of the by-products of scholarship that the choice of a subject tends to push toward partisanship. After all, if I am early into the field with my review of, say, crime-victim compensation programs, or methadone maintenance regimens, or determinate-sentencing legislation, it is to the advantage of my career—not to mention my purse—if the matter secures a firm hold on the public agenda. Few of us are interested in pursuing issues that will be stillborn or short-lived, unless we do so because we believe strongly that their expiration—to which we want to contribute—is for the best.

Despite such considerations, the authors of this book are able to maintain an even-handed and tentative stand in regard to house arrest. They express the standard reservations of sophisticated criminologists that the record of their discipline is replete with well-intentioned ideas that, with time, have been shown to be repressive, sometimes monstrously so. They regard their work as something of a blueprint, an early attempt to assess the multitudinous aspects of a complicated new social policy. They are wary that house arrest has the potential for "turning a person's home into a surrogate jail" and that, therefore, it represents "perhaps the ultimate audacity of the state." But they are not certain whether this is merely rhetoric, a visceral reaction to something ominously novel. After all, the unusual degree of housing privacy that exists in America is a luxury not widely shared in the civilized world. On the other hand, is Stanley Cohen, an eminent criminologist, correct when he warns that the broader move toward community corrections is blurring things, turning the community itself into one vast prison?

The authors promise that they intend to reexamine some of the fundamental issues after house arrest has been around longer and we must stand grateful for this continuing interest and concern. Meanwhile, the present volume offers an excellent and thorough introduction to a social movement of utmost importance, not only from a correctional viewpoint, but in terms of some of the fundamental concerns of any society seeking to remain free and democratic, and, as part of that aim, striving to treat its law offenders with decency and fairness.

Gilbert Geis

REFERENCES

Beaumont, Gustave de and Alexis DeTocqueville 1833/1964 *On the Penitentiary System in the United States and Its Applicability to France.* Francis Lieber (trans.). Carbondale: Southern Illinois University Press.

Dickens, Charles 1848 *Dombey and Son.* London: Bradbury & Evan. 1861 *Great Expectations.* London: Chapman and Hall.

Dryden, John 1669 *The Wild Gallant.* London: H. Heringman.

Emerson, Ralph Waldo 1856 *English Traits.* Boston: Phillips, Samson.

Gibbon, Edward 1776 *The Decline and Fall of the Roman Empire.* 2nd ed. London: Strahan.

Hale, Matthew 1736/1773 *The History of the Pleas of the Crown.* 7th ed. London: Tobey.

Honoré, Tony 1978 *Tribonian.* Ithaca: Cornell University Press.

Lambard, William 1581 *Eirenarcha or of The Office of the Justices of the Peace.* London: Ra. Newbery and H. Bynneman.

Latham, Robert and William Matthews 1971 *The Diary of Samuel Pepys.* London: G. Bell.

Scott, Samuel P. (ed.) 1932 *Corpus Juris Civilis: The Civil Law.* Cincinnati: Central Trust Co.

Semayne's Case 1604 5 Coke's Reports 91.

Turner, J. W. Cecil 1966 *Kenny's Outline of Criminal Law.* 9th ed. Cambridge: Cambridge University Press.

Watson, Alan (trans. & ed.) 1985 *The Digest of Justinian.* Philadelphia: University of Pennsylvania Press.

Weinberg, Kenneth G. 1971 *A Man's Home, A Man's Castle.* New York: McCall.

Preface

Our interest in "house arrest" as a correctional alternative began in 1980 as part of a search for some means of dealing with the pressing problem of jail and prison overcrowding. On the one hand, it seemed clear that the advocates of rehabilitation were in retreat and that it was simply unrealistic to expect a fair hearing for suggestions along those lines. The "lock 'em up" attitude was in full swing. Yet it was obvious that jail and imprisonment were unnecessarily harsh measures subject to proper criticism from "liberals" and that many of the "conservatives" allied with the trend toward increased incarceration were going to have second thoughts when the bills came due. But if one side of our interest in house arrest was essentially defensive, resting on the hope of finding a less severe and less expensive alterantive that would still satisfy the hue and cry for retribution, the other side represented a more positive aim. That is, we hoped to develop an alternative that would place more options in the hands of attorneys representing convicted offenders who were mentally impaired, terminally ill, or characterized by some other set of circumstances that would justify the filing of a petition requesting that the sentence be served in the home.

We encountered immediate opposition. Some dismissed the entire proposition out of hand as simply inconceivable. Others reacted with horror based, insofar as we could judge, on the association of the phrase *house arrest* with political repression abroad. We had our own reservations. One had to do with the very real possibility that this "alternative," like so many others, would become another means for extending the reach of the juvenile and criminal justice systems into the lives of citizens. And in addition to the danger of "widening the net," there was the possibility for even harsher repression than might be found in some jails and prisons, especially if electronic surveillance and control devices were to get out of hand.

Two of the authors tried to address these possibilities by seeking to implement the house arrest alternative through specific legislation rather than administrative fiat. This effort was focused in Kentucky, where a foundation of interest and legislative support had been built. Although Florida was to become the first state to pass legislation into which house arrest could be fitted as a correctional alternative, the Kentucky law, which we will describe, has tended to become the model.

In presenting this introduction to house arrest as a correctional alternative, we have several goals in mind. First, we believe it important to place this policy alternative in a broad, historical context so that its implications can be considered and debated in terms of the most general historical and philosophical concerns. Having done this, we will seek to introduce the reader to several specific house arrest programs, examining some of them in detail. Next must come a careful look at both the key legal issues surrounding this alternative and the most salient social and psychological issues that can be discerned at this point. Finally, we will move to certain tentative conclusions, considering both the promise and the peril of house arrest.

We would like to make our position clear. We regard house arrest as a promising possibility that should be closely examined and vigorously debated. But we continue to have some serious reservations. Whether these reservations are justified, time will tell. Rather than speculate too much here, our intention is to continue empirical work that can provide evidence with which to evaluate this new correctional policy.

Because this book examines a number of house arrest programs in different states and is based upon work conducted with the help of many others over a period of more than five years, our indebtedness is wide and deep. Space limitations prevent us from expressing our gratitude except to say thanks to the following people and organizations: Professor James Byrne, University of Lowell; Professor J. Michael Hunter, Northern Kentucky University; Professor Joseph Ohren, former Chair, Department of Public Administration, Northern Kentucky University, now of Eastern Michigan University; Professor Francis T. Cullen, University of Cincinnati; Provost Lyle A. Gray and Dean Darryl G. Poole, both of Northern Kentucky University; Kenton County's (Kentucky) District and Fiscal Courts; Diane Lehman and Kentucky's Department of Correction; Joseph B.

Vaugh, Sam Houston University; Lt. Eugene Garcia and Sergeant Art Davis, Palm Beach County Sherrif's Office; Fred Rassmusser and Beverly Auerbach, Pride, Inc., West Palm Beach, Florida; Glen Rothbart and Robert Thomas, *Correction Services*, Incorporated, West Palm Beach, Florida.

We are indebted to a number of individuals and organizations for their assistance with the juvenile justice portion of our research. We thank the Ohio Governor's Office of Criminal Justice Services and its Director, Mr. Michael Stringer, for funding that portion of the research. For her invaluable assistance with data collection and analyses, we acknowledge the efforts of Ms. Susan Filer Ballinger. Mr. Carl Sanniti (Director) and the staff of the Cuyahoga County (Ohio) Home Detention Project were very cooperative and generous with their time throughout the study. And finally, we appreciate greatly the assistance of the many juvenile court judges and court personnel who cooperated with our research efforts (especially those of the Cuyahoga County Juvenile Court, where many of our "case study" data were collected).

We extend our deep appreciation to our respective spouses, Helen, Pat, and Cindy, for their warmth, love, and understanding.

R.A.B.
C.R.H.
J.R.L.

1

The Rise of Institutional Incarceration and the Search for Alternatives

Recent years have seen a dramatic explosion of interest in the development of what has been referred to traditionally as *house arrest.* This term is often used very loosely, and it is probably preferable to refer to this correctional policy alternative as *home confinement,* a term that has the virtue of covering more specific practices, such as *home detention* (in which the residence is used as a detention facility) and *home incarceration* (in which the residence replaces a jail or prison as a place of incarceration). The term *house arrest* tends to imply police action without much in the way of judicial due process. Nevertheless, the term may be appropriate in a nontechnical sense because it offers a means of communicating the policy to the general public, a starting point in an effort to communicate more precisely the exact nature of this correctional alternative.

Home confinement has been both praised and damned. It has been praised as (1) more humane and less "corrupting" than confinement in a correctional institution and (2) most promising as an economical alternative to building more jails and prisons. It has been condemned, or at least seriously questioned, because it seems to turn the home into a prison, setting a dangerous precedent and violating the sanctity of one's home as one's "castle," a last refuge from governmental intrusion. In this chapter we will examine the historical context in which house arrest has suddenly become so popular. In the following chapters we will take a close look at several current programs, consider the major legal and social issues surrounding house arrest, and review the general policy implications and the potential future of this alternative.

Until about the middle of the twentieth century, it could be said that European history had shown three fairly distinct periods in the punishment of offenders (Rusche, 1933). This tradition was brought to North America. It is our contention that the past two decades have seen a major historical shift, with both Europe and North America moving into a fourth phase of what is now called correctional policy, and that the recent house arrest movement is part of this new phase. If we limited ourselves to the role of correctional technicians it might be possible to ignore all this and merely proceed to the "practical" question of whether the policy "works" or "fails." But there is a larger obligation. At least some effort must be made to understand where we have been and where we may be going.

During the early Middle Ages, offenders were punished almost exclusively by undergoing voluntary penance through physical suffering or payment of fines. The acceptance of punishment often followed a confession to religious authorities, such as a priest, with the offense defined as a *sin* and the penance as a symbolic repair for the wrongdoing. Such policy was consistent with the social conditions of the time. Reality itself was defined primarily in terms of religious conceptions of the sacred and profane. The population was stable, land was readily available, and laborers were needed. Aside from the nobility and the clergy, wealth was distributed rather evenly. Crimes tended to be the product of "the primitive stirrings of sexuality and hatred" rather than of economic motivation (Rusche, 1933). A peasant had no need to steal from a neighbor what he could produce himself, and there was little thought of excluding offenders from the community.

By the late Middle Ages, social conditions had changed considerably in Europe, and the punishment of offenders had entered a second phase. The population had expanded significantly, and available land had been settled. A quasi-capitalistic economic order had developed, and so had a host of social problems familiar to us today, including unemployment, crowded living conditions, low wages, and new crime problems. Property crimes became more common as hordes of beggars, thieves, and "rabble" crowded within the cities. Religious authority was being supplanted by secular authority, and fines were of little use because the poor had no money or possessions with which to pay. Traditional means of punishment gave way to new techniques as attention was directed toward the body of the offender (Foucault, 1977). Public whipping, branding, mutilation, and execution became the nearly universal means of punishment as the most gruesome tortures were applied to the body.

Some cities gibbeted portions of the body on high posts outside the city walls, forewarning what awaited evildoers should they violate the laws (Lofland, 1973). Sometimes the physical remains would be soaked in tar so they would last a long time as a warning to potential offenders (Andrews, cited in Sutherland and Cressey, 1978: 311). As late as the fifteenth century, England had only 17 capital offenses, most of which were of a religious nature. By 1780, however, there were 350 capital crimes, most of which were for property offenses, some so seemingly trivial as burning a haystack (Pollock and Maitland, 1968). In place of religion, a "property-conscious oligarchy" had assumed power, defining reality and molding the criminal law in terms of its concerns (Hay et al., 1975: 13).

The early signs of what was to become a third phase in the punishment of criminals can be found in the "houses of correction" that appeared in Calvinist Amsterdam in 1596, near the end of the Middle Ages (Sellin, 1944). Here the city burghers sought to introduce labor and religious instruction as a means of correcting offenders. This development was associated with an expansion of trade and the growth of new markets outside Europe at a time when plague and war had decimated the population, creating a shortage of labor. Although physical cruelty continued as the most popular means of punishing offenders, a new "humanitarianism" had begun to appear, a "humanitarianism" that happened to be perfectly consistent with the "work ethic" appropriate to the new economic order being born. Central to this "work ethic," which was to be a means of transforming rural peasants and urban rabble into a disciplined labor force of "willing workers," was a preoccupation with the concepts of "discipline" and "time." The general goal was expressed in the name given to the workhouses, *Tuchthuis,* which means "house of discipline."

Development of new markets overseas and exploitation of raw materials to be found there were major factors motivating the explorations of the fifteenth and sixteenth centuries. In England, it gradually became clear that control of North America depended upon the establishment and defense of permanent settlements. But it was not so easy to persuade settlers to make such a move, despite the land grant policies and provisions for free transportation and employment for several years as indentured servants. Beginning in the late

sixteenth century (1597), England authorized transportation to the
colonies as an alternative sentence for convicted offenders, a policy
that was deemed so successful in adding settlers that it was expanded
in 1718 to include all criminals who had been sentenced to three or
more years of imprisonment (Bowker, 1982). Most European countries
followed England's lead, France beginning transportation in earnest
in 1791 and Russia embracing the policy on such a grand scale that
being "sent to Siberia" became synonymous not only with penal
transportation, but with almost any form of social banishment.

The themes of discipline and scheduling were interwoven in
transportation policy through imposition of forced labor on the
convicts and setting of length of sentences, both of which were
measurable. So much work had to be accomplished within a
particular period of time, and strict planning and control allowed for
the carefully rationalized planning for economic ventures, such as
road building and forestry or quarry work (Johnson, 1978). Transportation continued in North America until the Revolution, by which
time the colonists had learned to resent the convicts being sent into
the colonies, and had discovered that African slaves could be
controlled and exploited more easily than English convicts could be
(Bowker, 1982). England shifted the direction of its transportation
policy to Australia, where convicts could be placed in penal colonies
or assigned to settlers for a period of as much as eight years before they
became eligible for a "ticket of leave." The new definition of the
punished body as an object, a commodity like any other that could be
bought and sold, "disciplined," "corrected," and exploited for profit
at the same time, is perhaps especially clear in the policy by which
individuals could contract with European governments to transport
convicts who could then be sold for periods of servitude ranging from
3 to 14 years (Taft and England, 1964). This application of private
enterprise to the "solution" of correctional problems is as old as
capitalism itself.

Transportation, however, was only an interlude in the historical
development of European punitive policy toward offenders as it
moved from a religious orientation, expressed through notions of
expiation through penance, to a more secular orientation, stressing
the inflicting of pain or death to the body, and then to the concept of
imprisonment in a tightly controlled environment designed to
remake the offender into a disciplined laborer. And there was

considerable overlap among the three basic phases, especially in the colonies of North America. Penal institutions existed in the colonies, but they were uncommon for many years, partly because of lack of construction and maintenance funds and partly because the concept had not been fully accepted. Colonial policy was still heavily influenced by the religious orientation as expressed in Puritan codes in general and by the approach of the Pennsylvania Quakers in particular (Barnes, 1969). The first code of the New Haven colony states: "If any person within this Government shall by direct, express, impious or presumptuous ways, deny the true God and His attributes, he shall be put to death" (Barnes, 1969: 44). This code, drafted in 1642, as well as the Hempstead, Long Island, code of 1664, specified 11 capital offenses, including denying God, engaging in consenting homosexual acts between males over 14 years of age, and copulation with animals.

It is interesting to note that the Puritan codes tended to combine a preoccupation with religious offenses and a policy of inflicting corporal punishment or death on the offenders rather than adhering to the Catholic tradition of penance, which had predominated during the first phase of penal policy in Europe. While denying God or engaging in especially sinful sexual practices brought the death penalty, lesser crimes such as fornication were punished by a combination of fines, corporal punishment, branding, and the use of the pillory and stocks (Barnes, 1969). The tendency for increased harshness is also evident here, however, as the use of the death penalty was extended. By 1718 the Pennsylvania criminal code punished all felonies except larceny with death. The Quaker code of 1682 had included only one capital offense, premeditated murder, with the Quakers arguing that corporal punishment should be replaced with "the practice of imprisonment at hard labor" (Barnes, 1969: 190). But the British required loyalty oaths, which the Quakers refused to take, leading to a British refusal to recognize the Quaker code and an eventual compromise in which the Quakers accepted the "imposed" code of 1718 in return for the right of affirmation in lieu of the loyalty oath. The code of 1718 remained in effect until after the Revolution, at which time the former colonies were to enter the third of the penal policy phases described by Rusche (1933) as characteristic of European history—with the accent on imprisonment.

THE DEVELOPMENT OF IMPRISONMENT
IN THE UNITED STATES

As indicated above, it is our contention that house arrest or home confinement, as it is more properly designated, is part of a fourth phase in the development of European-North American punitive policy. This fourth phase amounts to a reaction against the third phase, the widespread transition to incarceration of convicted criminals within the walls of penal institutions. Assessment of home confinement within the context of this fourth phase of what is now called correctional policy depends to some extent upon one's assessment of the history of the imprisonment phase to which it is considered an "alternative." Unfortunately, there are competing accounts of the forces behind the development of imprisonment in the United States, just as there are differing opinions as to whether the basic purpose of the new policy was really reformation of the criminal, simply a different form of deterrence, merely a means of incapacitation for a period of time, or perhaps only another and somewhat more hypocritical technique of retribution in a society becoming uncomfortable with overt public torture in the form of corporal punishment and hanging.

The conventional explanation for the development of imprisonment in the United States focuses upon the humanitarian concerns of the Quakers, who argued against corporal punishment, wished to limit capital punishment in favor of imprisonment, yet were appalled by the horrible conditions of the jails in colonial New England (Mitford, 1974). According to this account, the Quakers placed Pennsylvania in the forefront of penology shortly after the Revolution, with reforms that were a reaction against the British policies and a response to the writings of reformers such as Montesquieu, Voltaire, Diderot, Beccaria, Paine, and Bentham (Barnes, 1969; Bowker, 1982). This interpretation of events stresses the early reforms enacted at the Walnut Street Jail in Philadelphia, a chaotic "scene of promiscuous and unrestricted intercourse, and universal riot and debauchery" (Gray, quoted in Sutherland and Cressey, 1978: 520). Prisoners did not labor, nor were they given any form of instruction or "discipline." Conditions were so bad that some died of starvation. The Quakers reacted with the creation of a reform association named the Philadelphia Society for Alleviating the Miseries of Public Prisons.

Despite the prominence of the Quakers in the prison movement, there is much evidence to suggest that the basic thrust behind the trend was quite similar to that which had given birth to the *Tuchthuis* two centuries earlier. The Tuchthuis was different from the jail. It was above all else a place that was *organized*. It was a place of discipline, routine, and work. This new phase was not to come into its own in the United States. As several students of the change have pointed out, the "reforms" were a product of changing production relationships that had been set in motion in Europe and in the colonies before the Revolution (Sellin, 1970; Smith and Fried, 1975; Takagi, 1975). Some have argued that the "reforms" were actually importations of British policy rather than post-Revolutionary Quaker innovations. Jails had been established under British rule as early as 1635, although it is true that they were too small to hold many prisoners and poorly maintained. Workhouses ("bridewells") had been established by approximately 1655, almost exactly a century after their establishment in England. The major difference between Quaker preferences and British policy seems to have revolved around the question of prison labor, with the Quakers advocating solitary confinement without labor as conducive to the moral regeneration of prisoners who would use the time to contemplate their wrongdoing and seek a more spiritual direction, and the British policy stressing discipline through labor.

The Quaker position is most clearly exemplified by what came to be known as the Pennsylvania System, an approach that is, in turn, best illustrated by the construction and operation of the Eastern State Penitentiary in Philadelphia, a model institution developed after the failure of the Western State Penitentiary, which had been built in Pittsburgh in 1827. Here the prisoners were kept in solitary confinement; an inmate could spend an entire sentence in a cell, seeing only prison officials and those who brought meals (Johnson, 1978). British policy was more apparent in the so-called Auburn System, named after a different sort of practice being developed simultaneously at a new prison in Auburn, New York. Here prisoners were allowed to congregate for industrial production in shops within the prison walls during the workday and were returned to their cells at night. The major defect of the Pennsylvania System lay in the severe physical and mental deterioration of prisoners forced to serve a lengthy sentence with virtually no human contact. The major defect of the Auburn System involved the combination of extremely hard work with a demand for total discipline and perfect obedience backed by frequent corporal punishment, especially for violations of the rule of strict silence (Gibbons, 1982; Johnson, 1978).

A look behind the scenes of the struggle for preeminence between the Pennsylvania System and the Auburn System can be very revealing. Prior to their intense involvement with conditions at the Walnut Street Jail and their later involvement with the construction of the Western State Penitentiary and then the "model" Eastern State Penitentiary, the Philadelphia Society for Alleviating the Miseries of Public Prisons, with the support of Benjamin Franklin, had called for a change in punishment policy that would require "hard labor, publicly and disgracefully imposed." According to this plan, prisoners were to work on roads or other public works with shaved heads and special clothing identifying them as convicts. It was less than two years later that the same society recommended to the Pennsylvania legislature that "punishment be more private or even solitary labor."

The shift in punishment policy from penance or corporal/capital punishment of offenders to imprisonment has been described as a transition from a policy of "inclusion" dealing with them in the community to one of "exclusion," by which they were punished through incarceration outside the community (Cohen, 1985). Why the change in the position of the society that had less than two years earlier recommended public labor? The problem was that the overt, public exploitation and degradation of the prisoners often generated fights and even riots on the part of the outraged family and friends of the offender. Such treatment was also reminiscent of the British practice of exploiting political prisoners, a practice that had greatly angered the colonists only a few years before. After the brief trial of "hard labor, publicly and disgracefully imposed," it was apparently deemed more prudent to move toward a policy of exclusion that had the merit of putting a wall between the infliction of the punishment and the eyes of the community.

But given the Quaker position on hard labor, what explains the advocacy of "labor," first "publicly" and then "more private" by the society? The apparent answer is that Quaker membership in the society may have been outnumbered by Episcopalians, who did favor both solitary confinement and hard labor (Takagi, 1975). That the later position taken by the society was less a "Quaker" position than an "Episcopalian-British" position is suggested by various pamphlets circulated at the time, one of which states quite clearly that "exactly

what was needed at home was to follow the English example"
(Takagi, 1975). It is worth noting that the Pennsylvania legislature
reacted to the recommendation for "more private or solitary labor" by
requesting more information and asking for assurance that the policy
would both produce "willing labor" and turn a profit. Upon receipt
of additional information and assurances, the legislature had in 1789
provided that any felon convicted in Pennsylvania and sentenced to
12 months of hard labor *might* be sent to the Walnut Street Jail, and
appropriated 100 pounds per year for maintenance. Slightly more
than a year later the famous law implementing solitary confinement
at hard labor was passed. This 1790 law had set the precedent by
ordering separation of the sexes at the jail, constructions of cell
blocks, and imprisonment at hard labor for *all* so-called hardened
criminals. By 1794 the law required that all offenders convicted in
Pennsylvania *had* to be sent to the Walnut Street Jail, effectively
transforming it from a local jail to a state prison. Within a few years,
the Quakers had been removed from the governing board of the jail
and had formed an *opposition* group that campaigned for solitary
confinement *without labor*. Thus even in Pennsylvania the image of
"reforms" sparked by humanitarian Quakers is somewhat deceptive.
It would appear that the real struggle amounted, in the long run, to a
question of whether or not the hard labor was to be performed in
solitary confinement or in the officially silent company of other
prisoners.

The Auburn System had several advantages in the eyes of the
authorities. Perhaps its major advantage, however, was its more
"modern" appearance. The system in use in Pennsylvania, whether
the pure form of the Quaker-inspired Pennsylvania System of solitary
confinement *without* labor or the modified system of solitary
confinement *with* labor, seemed to many outmoded in comparison to
the up-to-date Auburn System. The pure system of solitary confinement without labor appeared to be an expensive coddling of
prisoners, and even the modified system of solitary confinement with
labor smacked more of the outdated practice of a "cottage industry"
rather than the efficient "factory system" in use at Auburn. Why not
have the convicts at work in modern "shops" in company with fellow
workers, with the "contamination" of prison talk contained by
careful management of prisoner time and disciplined silence? The
sight of dozens of convicts moving in silence in these shops might call
to mind the original *Tuchthuis* model of a "house of discipline"

where human interaction was completely forbidden and machinelike labor was successfully employed to the twin ends of correcting the offender and profiting the state.

The destructive effects of prison life were, however, apparent from the beginning. Nevertheless, the concept had such a powerful grip over the minds of the authorities, and later the public, that efforts at "reform" were largely confined to modifications in the nature of imprisonment itself rather than to possible abolition. In the late 1860s and 1870s, for example, "reformatories" were constructed for youthful offenders on the idea that the institution might *create* changes in offenders, rather than wait for them to change as a result of reaction to prison life. The notion of the indeterminate sentence appeared in New York in 1869 and was endorsed by the American Prison Conference of 1870, coming from England through the Irish system (Gillin, 1935). Parole had already been introduced in the 1830s as a form of conditional release under the old "ticket of leave" philosophy and was gradually expanded with the creation of parole boards charged with determining whether inmates were ready for release at a particular point. None of these efforts at "reform" represented a major policy shift.

As Austin and Krisberg (1981) have noted, it is the common fate of new departures to be caught in the "dialectics of reform." They are offered by those seeking some fundamental change, but if accepted are applied in actual practice in accordance with the dictates of the old order as it has been structured traditionally. Thus once imprisonment had become the new norm, attempts to introduce more "creative" practices through the "reformatories" tended to be stifled by the assumption that security, discipline, and hard work must be considered primary. The indeterminate sentence became a coercive tool by which inmates could be motivated to (1) avoid attempts at escape, (2) submit to the strict discipline with minimum complaint, and (3) labor hard and willingly, all in the hope of an earlier release date. Like the indeterminate sentence, parole also became something of a tool for the more efficient management of the prison rather than a fundamental shift in the nature of the policy of imprisonment. Parole boards proved to be very conservative, releasing very few prisoners before the end of their maximum sentence.

By 1900 imprisonment was a firmly established policy with widespread support. The years between 1900 and 1935 saw a 140%

increase in the prison population of the United States (Allen and Simonson, 1986), something that was to happen again in more recent years. The result was overcrowding. Prisons were reported to be 11.7% over capacity in 1926 and 19.1% over capacity in 1927 (Tannenbaum, 1938). In some states the problem was much greater: North Carolina reported its prison system at 135.2% above capacity in 1932, meaning that the institutions in that state held more than twice the number of inmates for which they had been constructed. Although some caution must be exercised here because of the different definitions of *capacity* used by different wardens, it is clear that prison overcrowding had become a significant problem despite the construction of many more institutions.

The reaction was quite different from that of recent years, which have also seen a rapid rise in the prison population and serious problems of overcrowding contributing to a vigorous search for "alternatives." The primary explanation is to be found in the fact that the adult institutions of the time were essentially self-sustaining industrial prisons, often actually earning a profit. But this was to change as the newly influential labor movement began to challenge such prisons on grounds of unfair competition based on virtually free labor from the convicts. A series of state-level modifications in prison labor practices was already under way when in 1929 the U.S. Congress passed the Hawes-Cooper Act, which required that prison products be subject to the laws of any state to which they were shipped, and the later Ashurst-Summers Act, which essentially stopped interstate transportation of prison products (Allen and Simonsen, 1986).

These changes were to the advantage of union labor, but for prison inmates they meant that prisons now became "monuments to idleness, monotony, frustration, and repression," one consequence of which was a "wave of riots" in the years between 1929 and 1932 such as had never before occurred in prisons in the United States (Allen and Simonsen, 1986: 50). Altogether, there were more than 400 known prison uprisings between 1855 and 1955 (Fox, cited in Mitford, 1974: 250), but never had they been so common. While prison rioting subsided during World War II, it reemerged during the postwar years, with more than 100 riots reported between 1950 and 1966 and very likely many more that went unreported by prison administrators dependent upon legislative funding and an image of good order in their institutions.

PHASE FOUR:
ALTERNATIVES TO INCARCERATION

By the 1960s it had become clear that the policy of exclusion, which punished the offender by incarceration within a secure penal facility, troubled by idleness, overcrowding, and inadequate financial support, was ill conceived. Inmates began to organize, and in some cases to riot, in an effort to call attention to their grievances. Some changes were made as a result of state and federal legislative reforms and decisions handed down by the U.S. Supreme Court. It is important to realize that all this took place during a major civil rights movement. To a considerable extent, what was happening in jails and prisons was a reflection of what was happening in the larger society. Many state legislatures created new programs, including educational programs, work release, home furloughs, and other innovations, all of which required additional funds. The period of the 1960s and early 1970s witnessed an extension of prisoners' rights and the application of constitutional guarantees to the states. Incarceration became more expensive and more troublesome to administer.

Ironically enough, reported increases in crime rates throughout the United States in the late 1960s and 1970s led to a proliferation of "get tough" laws with harsher and less flexible sentences. Parole boards became more conservative, approving fewer and fewer paroles. The result of sending more offenders to jail or prison for longer periods of time while releasing fewer on the "other end" was predictable. Correctional institutions were subjected to severe over-crowding and tremendous social, legal, and economic pressures. From 1970 to 1979 the imprisonment rate increased an unprecedented 39% (Langan, 1985). This dramatic shift continued as the prison population in the United States jumped from 300,034 in 1977 to 463,866 in 1984 (Beck and Greenfield, 1985). It is now over 540,000.

Those faced with this problem perceived essentially two solutions. If imprisonment was to remain basic policy, then more institutions had to be built and maintained. If not, then it would be necessary to seek "alternatives to incarceration," and perhaps to move into a fourth phase in the European-North American tradition of punishing offenders. As was often the case in the past, a new direction was taken without abandoning the old. Many correctional facilities were constructed. There were, for example, 31 more state prisons and one more federal prison in 1984 than in 1983 (Allen and Simonsen, 1986). But there are limits to the former policy: One new prison cell may cost more than $80,000, and the yearly cost of holding each inmate may exceed $15,000. In some cases the costs are even higher. A Minnesota correctional institution has reported direct and indirect *daily* maintenance costs at $103 per inmate or a total of more than $36,000 per year, more than twice the amount it would have cost to send the inmate to Harvard (Cory and Gettinger, 1984). And other prison systems that have held down costs are faced with court orders to upgrade facilities and programs. Indeed, in some cases the courts have assumed control of state prison systems in judicial determination to implement the mandated improvements.

Despite the tendency to cling to and even to accelerate the old policy of *exclusion* of offenders in walled institutions, it seems clear that North America has entered a fourth phase of punitive policy, a phase that will lay heavy stress upon *inclusion* of the offender through what is usually termed *community-based corrections*. Of course, probation has been an "alternative" for many years, but probation has come under fire as amounting to mere "leniency" that neither punishes nor rehabilitates offenders but simply ignores them if they stay out of further trouble for a certain time. What was planned was nothing less than a "new justice" (Aaronson et al., 1977) that would provide alternatives in the form of halfway houses, weekend incarceration, diversion programs, restitution, and community service options, and a variety of other "community-based" strategies. Such alternatives have proved so popular in some circles that it can be claimed that "community corrections for the majority of offenders is the way of the future" (Allen and Simonsen, 1986: 63).

One of the most recent of these new "alternatives" is home confinement or house arrest and it is probably best understood within the larger context of the movement in a fourth phase of punitive policy, a phase that relies upon *inclusion* of the offender within the community. House arrest is a particularly dramatic example of the extent to which inclusion may develop in that it appears to take "community corrections" to the limit by converting the most private of realms, the home, into a place that actually *functions* as a correctional facility. Some have questioned the trend toward community corrections as another move toward repression under the guise of "humanitarianism," a policy that is having the effect of turning the "community" itself into one vast prison (Cohen, 1985). If this is true, then the movement toward "alternatives" is a continuation of the imprisonment phase of punitive policy rather than a new phase. This is a subject beyond the scope of the present volume. Our hope is that it can be addressed at length at another time, after the groundwork has been laid by an examination of some actual programs, a consideration of basic legal issues, and an effort to reach certain preliminary conclusions.

HOME CONFINEMENT

House arrest has a long history, but this history is a cause for concern among some because of the traditional use of the practice as a means of silencing political dissent. South Africa, for example, has a long history of control through "banning," and societies such as Poland, South Korea, India, and the Soviet Union are known to employ house arrest primarily to deal with troublesome political dissenters. On the other hand, France introduced the concept of *control judiciare* in 1970 as a fairly straightforward form of pretrial detention involving a provision that employed home confinement as an alternative for common offenders (Gerety, 1980). In 1975, Italy initiated a policy of *affidamento in provo ai servizio sociale* (trial custody), which may be described as a form of parole following a shock period of three months' incarceration, and other European countries have also experimented with some manner of home confinement as a means of dealing with a variety of offenders. The traditional use of house arrest should not in itself become a rationale for rejecting it.

In the United States, home detention had been put in practice in St. Louis as early as 1971 (Rubin, 1985), and by 1977 such programs for youth had been put in place in Washington, D.C.; Baltimore, Maryland; Newport News, Virginia; Panama City, Florida; St. Joseph-Benton Harbor, Michigan; and San Jose, California (Young and Papenfort, 1977), as well as in Louisville (Bowker, 1982) and Tuscaloosa County, Alabama (Smyka and Selke, 1982). These programs developed first as a means of dealing with youthful offenders within a context of home and family and were, in part, a response to widespread concern that juveniles were being detained in increasing numbers unnecessarily and unjustly in secure detention facilities prior to adjudication. In view of these concerns and the traditional use of such practices as curfews in dealing with troublesome youth, home detention seemed an attractive alternative, and it had the additional merit of economic appeal. These first home detention programs were in essence much like current forms of *intensive supervision* (Gettinger, 1983), proceeding on the assumption that youth can be kept out of further trouble by daily telephone contact and cooperation with parents and teachers (Young and Pappenfort, 1977). This trend will be examined more closely in Chapter 2, and a detailed examination of one current program, the Cuyahoga County Project, will be undertaken in Chapter 3.

The later movement toward home confinement of adult offenders was somewhat less the result of a desire to protect the offender from the "corrupting" and "stigmatizing" effects of institutional incarceration, although this was one major consideration in proposals for use of the practice with drunken drivers (Ball and Lilly, 1983b than it was a consequence of jail and prison overcrowding and the felt need for more careful supervision of offenders granted probation. In Florida, for example, the Correctional Reform Act of 1983 provided that confinement to one's residence was to be considered a diversionary alternative to incarceration and treated as an intermediate form of punishment—more strict than simple probation but less harsh than jailing or imprisonment. While Florida now has the most ambitious home confinement program in the United States, at least 30 states were implementing some form of house arrest by 1986, with another dozen states planning programs to be implemented within one year (Petersilia, 1986). The Florida programs will be examined in Chapter 4, where they will be compared to a current program in Kenton County, Kentucky.

Home confinement as a policy for use with adult offenders began to draw more attention in 1983, with the delivery of two different papers on the subject (Ball and Lilly, 1983a, 1983b), passage of the Correctional Reform Act, and the use of an "electronic bracelet" to monitor compliance with home confinement on the part of an offender in New Mexico (*Corrections Magazine,* 1983). The latter was inspired by a New Mexico district court judge's reading of a comic strip in which Spiderman was being tracked by a transmitter fixed to his wrist. The judge approached an engineer, who designed a device consisting of an electronic bracelet, approximately the size of a pack of cigarettes, which emitted a signal picked up by a receiver placed in a home telephone. This bracelet could be strapped to the ankle of an offender in such a way that if he or she moved more than 150 feet or so from the home telephone, the transmission signal would be broken, alerting authorities that the offender has left the premises. Officials in New Mexico gave approval for trial use of the device, and a research project funded by the National Institute of Justice eventually reported successful results with this "electronic monitoring" (Niederberger, 1984; Niederberger and Wagner, 1985).

The surge of interest in home incarceration of adults as an alternative to jailing or imprisonment has been closely associated with the development of this new technology. The policy began to receive more and more attention in academic circles (Ball and Lilly, 1984a, 1984b, 1985, 1986a, 1986b, 1987, Berry, 1985; Gable, 1986), corrections literature (Corbett and Fersch, 1985; Krajick, 1985), economic journals (*The Economist*, 1985: 90), criminal justice newsletters (*Criminal Justice Newsletter*, 1983, 1985a, 1985b), national newspapers (*New York Times*, 1985; *Wall Street Journal*, 1986), weekly news magazines (*Time*, 1985), electronic trade publications (*Electronics Week*, 1985: 30), popular magazines (*People*, 1985), national television (ABC, 1987), law journals (Goldsmith, 1983), criminal justice texts (Senna and Seigal, 1984), legislative reports (Legislative Record, 1985), and reports from the National Institute of Justice (Ford and Schmidt, 1985). Reports indicate that one company manufacturing electronic monitoring equipment saw that its "stock had just about quadrupled in price" two months after going public (Billitteri, 1986: 65) because of the perception of the "pioneering development of a new industry" (Brown, 1986).

Beginning March 3, 1986, the federal government approved an experimental program for the U.S. Bureau of Prisons, the Probation Service of the U.S. Courts, and the Parole Commission that would allow a federal parolee's release dates to be advanced 60 days on the condition that "he remain in his place of residence during a specified period of time each night" (*Federal Register*, 1986: 8903). Interest in home confinement had spread rapidly, and the reception was generally favorable. In the words of national television personality Barbara Walters, "Isn't it nice, finally, to be able to have a solution to something that seems sensible and that we should try to try more?" (*20/20*, 1986). At the same time, however, concerns were being expressed here and there. It seemed to some to be one thing to "ground" juveniles in home detention with daily contact supervision and assistance combined with official contact with parents and teachers, but another to treat adults "like children." Some who questioned home incarceration of adults felt that they should be jailed or imprisoned rather than "coddled," and others felt that turning a person's home into a surrogate jail was perhaps the ultimate audacity of the political state. The electronic monitoring devices, in particular, conjured up visions of some Orwellian nightmare in which the state might extend total surveillance over citizens. There is real confusion here (Lilly et al., 1986).

Two developments have added to the growing concern over the potential future of the house arrest movement. The first is the shift in the political climate; the second is the proliferation of technology. One's evaluation of the shift in the political climate during recent years is conditioned by one's reading of the history of corrections as outlined earlier. To some, this has been in general a story of *progress* from brutal torture to imprisonment and, finally, to community-based alternatives to incarceration. To others, the history is one of good intentions that have tended to produce unanticipated, *unfortunate consequences* at every stage. To still others, the shifts in punitive policy described above really represent deep and very insidious trends toward *total social discipline* and the complete suppression of individuality under the guise of humanitarianism and progress (Cohen, 1985). One's evaluation of the political climate that has emerged in recent years and one's views with respect to the newly powerful technology depend to some extent on the way past history is read.

Perhaps the best way to describe the recent "shift in the political climate" is to turn to Packer's (1968) work contrasting the two fundamentally different approaches to criminal justice, the *due-process model* and the *crime control model*. The 1960s was a time of powerful movements in the area of civil rights, and this was reflected in the policies of the legislative, executive, and judicial branches of the federal government. The "Warren Court," as the U.S. Supreme Court under Chief Justice Earl Warren was usually called during those years, moved toward the due-process model in a way that delighted some and outraged others. This approach stresses the rights of the accused and demands strict "due process" on the part of the government so as to protect the individual. The "Burger Court," under Chief Justice Warren Burger during the 1970s and into the 1980s, tended toward the crime control model (Hass and Inciardi,

1980), an approach that lays heavier stress on the "rights of society" and regards crime control as so important that greater state intervention is necessary.

The shift in the political climate that occurred in the late 1970s and continued into the 1980s appears to represent a backlash reaction to the rapid changes of the 1960s. With this shift came a sharp move to the conservative political right that witnessed the election of Ronald Reagan to the presidency and an increase in the number of conservatives elected to both houses of the federal government (Inciardi, 1984). In terms of the present volume, the most significant aspect of this shift is the way it may affect the nature of the legal and social boundaries between the public and private realms. The nature of these boundaries will be examined in some detail in Chapter 5.

To a considerable extent, concerns expressed over possible invasion of privacy, either by the government or by private agencies, have come because of the enormously increased power of technology to penetrate the private realm. The federal Office of Technology Assessment (1985) has called for immediate federal legislation to control this technology, indicating that (1) the extent and use of electronic surveillance by the private sector is unknown, (2) the number of federal court-approved wiretaps and hidden microphone "bugs" was in 1984 (the last year surveyed) the highest ever, (3) about 25% of the federal agencies responding to the 1984 survey indicated some use of electronic surveillance, and (4) a number of federal agencies were relying heavily upon such technology with the FBI, for example, using nine different types of surveillance technology in 1984 with plans to implement eight additional types as soon as it's feasible. In addition to new techniques in data transmission, "beepers," sensors, closed-circuit television systems, satellite communication equipment, electronic mail, cellular telephone equipment, miniaturized cameras, optical devices, and a host of other surveillance devices, the Office of Technology Assessment (1985) identified at least 85 computerized record systems operated by federal agencies for purposes of law enforcement, investigative, and intelligence matters. These systems together included about 288 million records covering approximately 114 million citizens.

As indicated above, one's evaluation of these developments and the shifting political climate of recent years may depend upon which reading or combination of reading of correctional history seems most plausible. For those who believe that all change is essentially "progress," there will be little here about which to be concerned. For those who see correctional history as a story of reasonable plans tending to produce unforeseen and often unfortunate consequences, the rise of house arrest in the political climate of the late 1970s and 1980s, combined with the potential misuse of the newly powerful technology, will most likely be viewed with some optimism and more than a little caution. For others who share a sense of a prevailing willingness of citizens to surrender their privacy to the state and to allow themselves to be subjected to greater and greater surveillance in return for a promise of security, both the political shift and the technological power now available to the state may mean that the rise of home confinement is perceived as another ominous sign.

Does house arrest represent "progress" as a genuine alternative to the harsh conditions of jail and prison? Is it a promising policy that must be given careful scrutiny because of certain latent dangers of going awry? Or are we witnessing a general decline of privacy and personal autonomy and a movement toward a society characterized by a passive and docile citizenry and devoted to maximum security through technological power (Marx, 1981)? In the following chapters we will examine some current examples of the use of home confinement ranging from home detention of youths in an effort to work with their parents and teachers to provide assistance to the increasing use of home incarceration with adults under a policy of electronic monitoring. We will devote considerable attention to the legal and social issues that must be faced in house arrest, especially if this new correctional policy is extended to more and more offenders. Although the policy is too new to allow for any firm conclusions at this point, certain preliminary conclusions and policy implications can be set forth and assessed.

2

House Arrest
and Juvenile Justice

Placing juveniles on house arrest, as an alternative to the use of secure detention facilities, has evolved in response to concerns about (1) the harmful effects of confining juveniles in adult jails, (2) the dysfunctional aspects of isolating youths from their families and from the communities in which they live, (3) the overcrowding that exists in many adult jails and juvenile detention centers, and (4) the absence of suitable facilities in many areas of the nation. The history of juvenile justice in America is filled with policy debates—even social movements—concerning the confinement of juveniles in jails and other secure detention facilities. The preadjudicatory detention of juveniles in a secure facility, analogous to holding an adult in jail prior to trial, has been the subject of numerous task forces and commissions, which have concluded that tight restrictions should be placed on juvenile detention practices.

JAILING JUVENILES:
A SUICIDAL POLICY?

The most severely criticized practice has been the use of adult jails to detain youths. A federal initiative to reduce this practice has won support, not only from child advocates, but from the National Association of Counties, the National League of Cities, and the National Sheriffs Association, among others (Rubin, 1985: 128). In addition to being concerned about the welfare of children locked up in such jails, these professional associations are also keenly aware of the problems involved in jailing juveniles—including inefficient use of jail space and the expanded personal liability they may face if a juvenile is victimized or commits suicide while in jail.

Nonetheless, approximately 500,000 youths are held in adult jails each year, about 60 of whom die before leaving jail (Rubin, 1985: 128). A recent national study found that the suicide rate for juveniles in adult jails is nearly five times greater than it is for juveniles in the general population, and nearly eight times greater than it is for juveniles held in separate juvenile detention centers (Community Research Center, 1980). This high suicide rate is a good illustration of how a well-intentioned policy can have unintended consequences. Federal policy mandating the separation of juveniles from adults "by sight and by sound" was intended to eliminate the assaults, rapes, and other abuses that had occurred as a result of the "commingling" of adults and juveniles in confinement. However, as is so often the case, the implementation of such policy reform often presents its own set of problems.

One of the authors has visited many adult jails, built in the late 1800s, where compliance with this federal policy means that when a juvenile is being held, he or she will be placed either in the basement of the jail or on its top floor. This isolation, intended to separate and protect the youth from older, perhaps more "hardened," inmates, also makes it almost impossible to supervise these isolated youths in understaffed jails.[1] Since youths held in jail following their arrest may be filled with feelings of guilt, remorse, or even self-hatred, it is not difficult to appreciate why the risk of suicide is dramatically elevated. The isolated location of these youths within the jail precludes both effective supervision and any meaningful opportunity to discuss their problems. Also, such facilities typically offer little or no programming for either youths or adult inmates. For example, when asked what the juveniles do for recreation, a jailer told one of the authors, "Oh, we take them out to the [country] fairgrounds and let 'em run once in awhile" (Huff, 1980)

From the efforts of the earliest advocates of a separate juvenile court in the 1890s to the present, reformers have argued for the removal of all juveniles from adult jails. The early efforts resulted in the establishment of specialized juvenile detention facilities. At first, these facilities indiscriminately mixed delinquents, status offenders, and dependent and neglected children. Then, in 1932, Cleveland established the first facility to employ a more sophisticated design that allowed for the segregation of subgroups with different needs (Rubin, 1985: 121). Thus the reformers had achieved a major goal: The establishment of a separate juvenile detention facility that segregated juveniles from adults and allowed for the additional separation of juveniles who presented different needs and different levels of risk. But what of the decision to detain, taken by itself? Were too many children and youths being locked up?

The Deinstitutionalization Movement

Although many areas of the nation still do not have separate detention facilities for juveniles (and many of those that *do* exist are inadequate), the focus of more recent reformers has shifted to advocacy for community-based *alternatives* to detention centers and jails. In the juvenile justice arena, this movement gained considerable momentum as a result of two pieces of federal legislation—the Omnibus Crime Control and Safe Streets Act of 1968[2] and the Juvenile Justice and Delinquency Prevention Act of 1974[3] (as amended in 1977)—both of which mandated the deinstitutionalization of status offenders. This means, in effect, that youths who are charged with, or who are found to have committed, "offenses" that would not be illegal acts if committed by an adult, shall not be confined in a secure detention or correctional facility (except, under certain conditions, for a period not to exceed 24 hours, or for having violated a valid court order).

The rationale for community-based alternatives to institutional confinement has at least some of its roots in a theoretical perspective commonly known as "labeling theory,"[4] which holds that the juvenile and adult justice systems, especially their correctional facilities, are themselves "criminogenic," or cause additional criminality and delinquency, by treating their "clients" as abnormal. According to this perspective, the stigma associated with these systems "marks" an individual in our society, thus reducing his or her chances of being accepted and leading a normal, noncriminal life.

Although the general validity of the labeling perspective has not been effectively demonstrated, it has great intuitive appeal and "face validity." Furthermore, the implications of labeling theory overlap significantly with the emphasis of those promoting the development of a "least restrictive alternatives" policy in the administration of juvenile justice. From the latter point of view, the least restrictive alternative should be used in each case, and secure detention should be reserved almost exclusively for those charged with or convicted of serious crimes, especially crimes against persons.

Consider, for example, the juvenile detention policy guidelines advocated by a joint task force of the Institute of Judicial Administration and the American Bar Association (see Appendix A). Detention, the task force said in Standard 6.6, should be limited to juveniles who are fugitives from justice or who are charged with violent felonies where commitment to a secure institution is likely if the offense is proven, and where one of the following additional factors is present:

(1) the crime charged is a class one juvenile offense;
(2) the juvenile is an escape from an institution or other placement facility where he was sentenced following adjudication for criminal conduct; or
(3) there is a recent record of willful failure to appear at juvenile proceedings, and no measure short of detention will reasonably ensure his appearance at court (Institute for Judicial Administration—American Bar Association, 1980).

These IJA-ABA *Standards*, as well as those promulgated by the National Advisory Committee for Juvenile Justice and Delinquency Prevention (1980), reflect a "least restrictive alternatives" policy preference, developed in response to the overcrowding, neglect, and abuse in many of the nation's detention facilities and jails.

HOUSE ARREST:
THE LEAST RESTRICTIVE ALTERNATIVE?

Just a few years after the catalytic Omnibus Crime Control Act of 1968, the nation's first house arrest program for juveniles was implemented in St. Louis. Since that beginning, in 1971, many additional programs—known variously as house arrest, home detention, or home supervision—have evolved, and most have been patterned after the programmatic model developed in St. Louis.

How do these programs work? Who staffs them? How are they structured? What are the major goals of these programs? What policy issues do they address? How successful are they? What does *success* really mean? What is their comparative cost? Who is referred to them and what criteria do they use to screen potential candidates for house arrest? Do they threaten public safety by keeping in the community juveniles who belong behind bars? Do they represent a true alternative to secure detention or do they merely expand the "net" of social control by focusing on youths who normally would have been placed on regular probation with less intensive supervision? All of these questions, and others, must be addressed if we are to make responsible policy choices in the controversial area of juvenile correction. Fortunately, some valuable descriptive and evaluative information on such programs is available (see, for example, Keve and Zanick, 1972; Young and Pappenfort, 1977; Swank, 1979; Rubin, 1979, 1985). In the remainder of this chapter, we shall review what is known about house arrest programs for juveniles in the United States. Then, in Chapter 3, we'll take a close look at a contemporary model program and find out why it seems to work so well.

HOW DO THESE PROGRAMS OPERATE
AND WHAT ARE THE RULES?

In Jefferson County (Louisville), Kentucky, house arrest is imposed on the youth and his or her parents or guardian. The probation officer is expected to discuss with the youth and family all conditions imposed by the court prior to their leaving court, to ensure that the youth and family have a contact at the agency 24 hours a day, and to check for compliance, "If the probation officer suspects for any reason that these conditions are not being adhered to" and "to inform the Court of any noncompliance" (Jefferson County Juvenile Probation Services, 1983).

The court order imposing house arrest (see Appendix B) specifies the conditions and exceptions concerning the youth's activities during the house arrest sanction, and makes clear that the youth is considered to be in detention status, just as if he or she were detained in the Youth Center, and that any violation of the order will result in a return to the Youth Center. The parents or guardian are expected to enforce the rules of house arrest; if they fail to do so and fail to notify the court concerning violations, they may be prosecuted for contempt of court or for contributing to the delinquency of a minor (Jefferson County Juvenile Probation Services, 1983).

The Jefferson County Juvenile Court may also impose home

supervision, if a juvenile and his or her family are thought to be in need of additional support services during the adjudicatory process. Workers supervising youths placed in home supervision status have a maximum caseload of five and are expected to (1) execute a contract (see Appendix C) with the youth and the parent or guardian prior to their leaving court, (2) have at least one face-to-face *and* one telephone contact with the youth, and (3) have at least one face-to-face *or* one telephone contact with the parent or guardian each week. These contacts are intended to enable staff to identify problems, monitor the youth's adjustment, and provide needed services. If a youth violates the provisions of the agreement, a conference is held to determine whether to return the youth to court for noncompliance.

According to Swank (1979), the San Diego Home Supervision Program began in 1976 with a grant from the State Office of Criminal Justice Planning to the San Diego County Probation Department. Prior to the implementation of this program, whenever Juvenile Hall was overcrowded, minors had been released at detention hearings under house arrest and advised to stay at home until their next hearing. There was one major problem with this arrangement: The youths were not monitored to see if they were complying with the court's order. This situation changed dramatically on March 14, 1977, when the first two juveniles were referred to the Home Supervision Program, which assured judges that youths referred to the Program would either stay at home as required or be taken into custody.

Despite the warnings given to these first two youths, less than a week passed before one of them was arrested for smoking dope in his bedroom with his buddies. While being returned to Juvenile Hall, the youth reportedly commented, "I didn't think you'd be coming. I've never seen a probation officer so much" (Swank, 1979: 50). The staff was apprehensive that this initial program failure might cause the referring judge to lose confidence in the program. Actually, just the reverse occurred. The judge was impressed that the probation officers were enforcing the court's orders. That incident stimulated judicial confidence in the program's accountability and helped fuel its subsequent growth.

Rapid growth of these programs can, in fact, present significant problems, and the San Diego program is a good example. Consider the fact that San Diego County is approximately the size of the State of Connecticut. Then contemplate the fact that in the early days of the program, two probation officers were responsible for supervising

youths throughout the County and that officers often carried
caseloads of 30 or so at any one time (Swank, 1979)! Nonetheless, with
the assistance of volunteers, the program was able to provide random
monitoring 24 hours a day and 7 days a week.

On January 1, 1977, the Dixon Bill,[5] having been enacted by the
California Assembly, officially became law. This law encouraged
increased community treatment and the separation of status offenders
from delinquents. It also required that all counties operate home
supervision programs as one type of community alternative to the use
of detention facilities. Further, the California Welfare and Institutions
Code (Section 628.1) required the probation officer to release a minor
from the detention center and place him or her on home supervision if
the probation officer "believes 24 hour secure detention is not
necessary in order to protect the minor or the person or property of
another, or to ensure that the minor does not flee the jurisdiction of
the court" (San Diego County Probation Department, 1986). Two
goals are mandated for such home supervision programs in
California: (1) to assure appearance at interviews and court hearings
and (2) to assure that the minor obeys the conditions of release and
commits no offenses pending disposition of the case.

Workers' salaries are essentially subsidized by the state and
caseloads may not exceed 10. When possible, supervising officers are
assigned to monitor youths in the same geographic area in which the
officers reside. San Diego County's commitments, in return for these
funds, are: (1) to maintain at least 80% of the minors in the community
without returning them to custody, (2) to personally contact each
minor at least once a day, and (3) to provide supervision for at least
800 minors who would otherwise be detained. Minors who do not
comply with the terms of home supervision may be arrested by
probation officers and returned to juvenile court for review and
possible placement in secure detention.

All seven of the early house arrest programs evaluated by Young
and Pappenfort (1977) were administered by juvenile court probation
departments. In general, these programs were staffed by parapro-
fessionals known as "outreach workers," "community youth leaders,"
or "community release counselors." Each staff member typically had
a caseload of five youths at any one time. All seven programs expected
their youth workers to exercise daily supervision and to keep their
charges "trouble free and available to the court" for their hearings.

Surveillance in these programs was accomplished primarily by daily personal contacts (at least one per day) with each youth, and daily telephone or personal contacts with the youths' parents, teachers, and (where applicable) employers. The youth workers who staffed these programs typically worked out of their automobiles and their own homes rather than at probation offices or court facilities. There was an effort to keep paperwork requirements to a minimum so the youth workers would have more time to be actively engaged in the supervision of their assigned cases. In fact, travel vouchers and handwritten daily activity logs often constituted the only significant paperwork required of these workers.

The youths placed in such programs typically had the program's rules of participation explained to them in the presence of their parents. These rules usually included:

(1) attending school;
(2) observing a specified curfew;
(3) notifying parents or work as to whereabouts at all times when not at home, school, or work;
(4) abstaining from drugs; and
(5) avoiding companions or places that "might lead to trouble."

In addition to these general guidelines, additional rules or conditions could usually be added as agreed upon by the parties involved. Written contracts setting forth these conditions were frequently used in these programs.

All seven programs were based on the rationale that close supervision would generally keep juveniles "trouble free and available to the court." Six of the seven programs also rested on another assumption: that this type of program would enable youth workers to provide needed services to youths and their families, thus increasing the probability of success. Some programs emphasized counseling and services more than others did, however, even going so far as to expect youth workers to try to achieve a "big brother" type of relationship with each youth supervised, sometimes combined with advocacy and involvement with the youths' parents. Youth workers in three of the seven programs organized weekly recreational or cultural activities for all youths placed in their respective programs.

Youth workers in these programs often coordinated their efforts to provide better services (for example, one worker "covering" or taking responsibility for another when necessary). In all seven programs, youths who did not adhere fully to program requirements could be taken to secure detention by program youth workers.

WHO IS REFERRED TO
HOUSE ARREST PROGRAMS AND
WHAT SCREENING CRITERIA ARE USED?

It is interesting that not one of the seven programs evaluated by Young and Pappenfort (1977) was designed exclusively for status offenders. Two programs accepted only alleged delinquents, while the other five included both alleged delinquents and status offenders. Most (5) of the programs served 200-300 youths per year, while the other two accepted just over 1,000 youths in the fiscal year preceding the evaluation.

A recent study by one of the authors found that in the State of Ohio, juvenile court judges responding to a statewide survey reported that they consider three factors to be the most important in screening candidates for house arrest:

(1) the seriousness of the alleged offense;
(2) the youth's previous record; and
(3) the home environment.

A second "cluster" of factors, though less important, are also taken into consideration. These factors include protection of the child, protection of others, population or crowding in the detention facility, school adjustment, and time of day when the alleged offense occurred. Judges reported that the recommendations of court staff, especially probation officers, are very important in the decision to use house arrest (Huff, 1986).

In the seven programs assessed by Young and Pappenfort (1977), burglary was the most frequent delinquency charge filed against program participants. When charges filed against program participants were compared with those filed against youths in secure detention facilities, the two populations were similar, except for homicide, aggravated assault, and rape (relatively infrequent and rarely released to such alternative programs). Most delinquency charges filed against program participants were judged to be moderately serious.

WHAT DOES *SUCCESS* MEAN
IN SUCH PROGRAMS AND
HOW SUCCESSFUL ARE THEY?

In attempting to assess program success, the key question is one of definition. What constitutes success? Should one consider it a success if a youth, while in home detention status, is not charged with any new *offenses* prior to adjudication? Or does success require that he or she complete the period of home detention without any violations of the home detention agreement? Or without having been returned to secure detention? Bear in mind that even if a youth violates the rules and is returned to secure detention, he or she is still available to the court, just as would have been the case had the youth been in the detention center the entire time. This question is somewhat similar to the distinction made between parole revocation for an alleged criminal *offense* versus revocation for a *technical violation* of parole conditions.

Depending on one's operational definition of success, the data reported by Young and Pappenfort (1977) indicate that home detention programs' "success rates" ranged from 71% to 98%. That is, if one defines success as having completed home detention *without incident* (the most restrictive possible definition of success), Young and Pappenfort's data indicate that the *least* successful programs in their sample were 71% successful. If, on the other hand, one adopts a more liberal definition of success (having completed home detention without any new alleged offenses), the *best* programs they evaluated attained a success rate of 98%. In addition, the San Diego program reports that it monitored 910 minors in Fiscal Year 1984 and had a "97%+" success rate (San Diego County Probation Department, 1986).

In all seven of the programs selected for Young and Pappenfort's (1977) national evaluation, the percentages of youths returned to secure detention for rules violations exceeded those returned for either alleged new offenses or for running away. This suggests that the quality of supervision in these programs was quite high. Also, because all of the youths returned to secure detention for rules violations did subsequently appear in court, one might argue that the preventive measures of returning them to detention should be viewed as a success (it may have prevented serious delinquency and the youth was still available to the court), rather than as a program failure. Indeed, return to secure detention is a planned option in all such programs.

It is noteworthy that those programs, designed exclusively for alleged delinquents, were as effective as those that accepted status offenders as well as delinquents (Young and Pappenfort, 1977), underscoring once more the fact that "offense categories" are often a poor proxy, for either past behavior or future risk. Indeed, the researchers concluded that additional youths could have been handled in home detention programs and other alternative programs, and that some courts were "unnecessarily timid" in referring youths to such programs (Young and Pappenfort, 1977: 31).

A recent Ohio study found that a sample of 2,708 youths released on house arrest in 1984, a total of 2,470, or 91%, successfully complied with the conditions imposed upon them during the period of conditional release and subsequently appeared for adjudication. In this study, technical violations again accounted for far more "failures" than did new allegations of offenses (Huff, 1986). Furthermore, 85% of the juvenile courts responding to the survey indicated that their experience with house arrest was either "good" or "very good," with none rating the results worse than "fair" (Huff, 1986).

Of course, not all youths placed on house arrest succeed. One who did not is described in an anecdote involving one of the most memorable (and humorous) apprehensions in the history of house arrest programs:

> A home supervision officer was chasing a violator who scaled a wall. When the officer also went over the wall, he realized he had stumbled into a nude swimming party. The quick thinking youth apparently shed his clothes and disguised himself as one of the guests. He was apprehended the following day (fully clothed and grinning ear-to-ear) [Swank, 1979: 51].

WHAT IS THE COMPARATIVE COST
OF THESE PROGRAMS?

According to Keve and Zanick (1972), the cost per child per day in the original (St. Louis) home detention program was $4.85, compared to $17.54 per child per day in the juvenile detention center. This approximate one-to-four cost advantage also characterized another early home detention program begun in Louisville, Kentucky, in 1975 (Rubin, 1979: 101). Huff's (1986) Ohio study of house arrest indicated that secure detention costs averaged $42.57 per day; nonsecure detention and other nonsecure placements cost an average of $280.07 per day; and that house arrest was the least expensive of these three categories at just $14.94 per day (about one-third the cost of secure detention).

CONCLUSION

In this chapter, we have considered the nature and evolution of house arrest programs for juveniles in the context of historical reform movements and the policy debates surrounding juvenile detention. The smoke from these fiery debates over what to do with "juvenile delinquents" has not yet cleared, with articulate proponents of "locking them up" squaring off against equally eloquent adversaries favoring policies that promote the use of "the least restrictive alternatives" and "community based corrections."

We have also presented an overview of what is known about house arrest programs nationally, based on available research findings. The corpus of this research, while encouraging to the proponents of house arrest as a viable alternative to secure detention, leaves unanswered many questions that must be resolved if we are to develop sound public policy. Like much of the program evaluation literature, what we have reviewed tends to concentrate on *aggregate* findings and general descriptions. We are left with a blurry picture of generally successful programs, but we don't come away knowing *why* they work, fail to work, or work for some and not others. Very little of what has been published helps us understand the *differential* effects of these programs on different subgroups of participants, the political contexts in which house arrest programs operate, the views of the judiciary who refer youths and the workers who supervise them, and other important matters.

In the next chapter, we attempt to address many unresolved issues by taking a close look at a house arrest program for juveniles that seems to work very well—so well, in fact, that it could readily serve as a national model for such programs. In evaluating this program, we'll be interested in exploring whether its success rate is really as high as it appears to be. If so, why? What makes the program work so well? And if it does work so well, what does the future portend for the expansion of such programs? What, if any, resistance to such expansion might be anticipated?

We'll also examine the issue of failure. Who fails? Are those who fail distinguishable in any way from those who succeed? What lessons can be learned from this model program?

NOTES

1. Such jails, many of them in rural counties, typically have neither sufficient staffing nor the equipment required for effective electronic monitoring inside the jail.

2. Omnibus Crime Control and Safe Streets Act of 1968, Public Law No. 90-351, 82 Stat. 204 (codified as amended at 42 U.S.C. Section 3701, et seq.).

3. Juvenile Justice and Delinquency Prevention Act of 1974, Public Law No. 93-415, 88 Stat. 1109 (1974).

4. Although typically referred to as "labeling theory," this is really a theoretical *perspective*, rather than a systematic theory, since it does not incorporate any explanation of the subject's illegal behavior *prior* to his or her involvement in the justice system (the behavior that led to the arrest). If "labeling effects" explain subsequent law violations, what explains the original law violations? Labeling "theory" is essentially silent on this point.

5. California Assembly Bill 3121, effective January 1, 1977.

3

A Model House Arrest Program for Juveniles

What Makes It Work?

It was August, 1981, and Cuyahoga County (Ohio) juvenile court officials were uncomfortable. Their discomfort was not entirely due to the hot weather in Cleveland—at least the breezes that blew in from Lake Erie provided refreshing relief from that. Their discomfort stemmed instead from the burgeoning population of the detention home. They had no interest in simply "warehousing" juveniles, yet the mushrooming detention population was threatening to outstrip all available resources. It was unclear how best to stem this growth. After all, numerous alternative approaches might be taken, each of which had its advocates.

A consultant group was hired to advise the Court about this problem. The consultants recommended that the Court implement a house arrest program modeled after similar programs in San Diego and elsewhere. The program that was developed, known as the Cuyahoga County Home Detention Project,[1] was initially funded via the Law Enforcement Assistance Administration (LEAA). Subsequent to the demise of the LEAA, the project's funding has come primarily from the State of Ohio (Amended Substitute House Bill 440). This program has grown rapidly, and served nearly 1,000 youths in the past year alone.

Having completed a general review of house arrest programs for juveniles in America, we must now move to the specific level of analysis and consider a prototypical program, how it works, and why

Authors' Note: We wish to express our appreciation to Susan Filer Ballinger for her assistance in the collection and analysis of data used in this chapter.

it seems to work so well. An evaluation of this program (Huff, 1986) indicates that in its five years of existence, the Cuyahoga County Home Detention Project has attained a very impressive "track record" of success. The question to be raised here is: "Why?" Is it really the model program it seems to be? If so, what makes it work so well?

First, let's take a close-up look at the program and how it works.

ADMINISTRATION AND STAFFING

Structurally, the program is an integral part of the detention home of the Cuyahoga County Juvenile Court. The program's director is responsible to the superintendent of the detention home. The director is administratively responsible for the operations of the program and for directing the other program employees. These include a senior home detention caseworker and six home detention caseworkers. The senior home detention worker is described as the "right-hand man" of the director and is in charge in the director's absence. In addition to these staff, the court has recently allocated a full-time secretarial position exclusively for this program.

INTAKE AND REFERRAL

The Home Detention Project can receive referrals at two points in the adjudicatory process (see Figure 3.1) for status offenders and delinquents (either alleged or adjudicated). Once a complaint has been filed with the court, a referral can be made to this program. The initial point of referral, then, is at intake, and this referral may be made immediately upon preparation of the complaint. In an innovative attempt to provide the program's staff with the legal authority to return a youth to the detention home if necessary, each juvenile is initially referred (and, technically, admitted) to the detention home prior to being assigned to a probation officer.

At that point, the probation officer reviews the case and may make a referral to the Home Detention Project. This is especially likely if, in the probation officer's judgment, the youth needs more supervision than is generally available to probationers. This type of referral, as

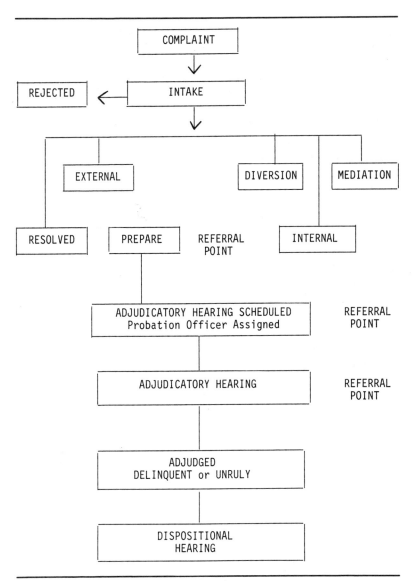

Figure 3.1: Referral Points for Home Detention

well as referrals from intake officers, is "preadjudicatory" (that is, it occurs prior to the court's adjudicatory hearing). While such pre-adjudicatory referrals initially dominated the program, the mix of referrals shifted quickly to a balance between pre- and postadjudicatory, then (in 1985) shifted dramatically toward postadjudicatory referrals.

A second referral point occurs when the youth appears for the adjudicatory hearing. At that point, of course, the judge would be the source of referral and the juvenile would be referred to the home detention project by the detention home. Such "postadjudicatory" referrals now comprise a majority of all referrals to the program. Both pre- and postadjudicatory referrals will be considered in this discussion, since both have important implications for the juvenile justice system.

Following referral to the program, the youths and their parents or guardian meet with the project supervisor to assess the appropriateness of the referral and the program's capacity to provide adequate supervision of the youths. Those youths not accepted in the home detention program are retained in the detention home until their court dates.

For those who are accepted, the next step involves discussing the behavioral guidelines the youths will be expected to observe. These conditions and expectations are embodied in a contract (see Appendix D), signed by the youths, their parents or guardians, and the project supervisor. The contract delineates both acceptable and unacceptable behavior, as well as the consequences of breaking the agreement. This contract, which was reviewed and approved by the County's attorneys prior to its use in the program, grants home detention workers the legal authority to return a youth to the detention home if necessary. The court retains legal jurisdiction over the children during the period of home detention (an average of about 17 days at present).

CASEWORKER QUALIFICATIONS
AND RESPONSIBILITIES

Following completion of the contract, youths are assigned to a home detention caseworker. Caseworkers generally have completed some college education, though a baccalaureate degree is not required. Instead, the project places great emphasis on relevant experience, including a minimum of two years child-care work or employment in a private placement facility. Caseworkers in this program are expected to be self-motivated, mature, responsible, and able to work independently. Home detention workers in Cuyahoga County typically are older than probation officers at the court. Once hired, these workers are required to complete a training course offered by the court, including conflict resolution, life space interviewing, and crisis intervention. Training is perceived as an ongoing need and continues as long as the worker remains employed in this program.

Home detention caseworkers have two primary responsibilities: (1) to see that the child appears in court for necessary hearings without any new arrests or infractions, and (2) to provide constructive alternative activities for each child. Activities designed to accomplish the latter goal range from having lunch with a youth to attending a sports event or simply sharing time in conversation. Caseworkers assist children in dealing with adjustment problems they may be experiencing at home or in school.

The primary method of intervention used by caseworkers is unscheduled, face-to-face contacts with the youth every day. In addition, the caseworker contacts parents daily, either in person or by telephone, and makes regular contacts with school personnel and employers, where appropriate.

Caseworkers' contacts concerning each child are recorded in the Daily Contact Log (see Appendix E) every day. This log enables the project to monitor each youth's behavior and compliance with his or her contract daily, and assists workers in writing final reports on each youth. In addition, the logs provide visible evidence that the caseworkers are maintaining these all-important daily contacts (we'll have more to say on the importance of these contacts later in this chapter).

In addition, youths are provided with School Report Forms (see Appendix F) and their teachers are asked to complete and sign these forms daily, thus providing a cumulative record of attendance, behavior, and progress (or lack thereof). Again, these forms serve multiple purposes. Not only do they document the youths' performance and behavior in school, but they also require school personnel to *verify* whether or not a specific youth is in attendance each day. Because many of the youths referred to the program have had poor attendance records and frequent tardiness, school personnel sometimes have assumed that if a youth wasn't in school on time, he or she would be absent for that entire day. The existence of this form, then, stimulates two-way accountability on the part of both the youth and the school.

Should the caseworker learn about, and act upon, a contract violation the caseworker completes a Violation Report (see Appendix G). This requirement provides documentation of such violations and discourages arbitrary, discretionary revocations of home detention (again, two-way accountability is built in). These forms are reviewed by the supervisor.

Prior to the court hearing, the caseworker completes the Home Detention Report (see Appendix H), a final report that is given to the judge or referee. This report summarizes the juvenile's home detention experience and is a valuable resource for the judiciary.

CLIENT POPULATION TRENDS

Tables 3.1 to 3.4 summarize the data concerning referrals and complaints filed, client population and service trends, and per diem costs. Clearly, the program has grown steadily, having provided supervision to 2,377 youths and nearly doubling in size between 1982 and 1985.

In terms of client population composition (Table 3.1) the referrals have been about equally divided between blacks and whites, with only occasional referrals of other clients. Approximately 60% of all referrals to the program have been males, 40% females. The average age of youths in the program has remained at about 15.

As reflected in Table 3.3, the average per diem cost to administer home detention has actually *dropped* steadily, from $24.25 in 1982 to

TABLE 3.1
Referrals to Cuyahoga County Home
Detention Project, 1982-1985

Year	Referrals
1982	408
1983	549
1984	662
1985	758

TABLE 3.2
Client Population Composition, Cuyahoga County
Home Detention Project, 1983-1985

Year	Sex		Race		Average Age
	Male	Female	Black	White	
1983	328	221	311	333	15.33
1984	412	250	332	330	15.06
1985	432	326	372	286	15.16

$13.44 in 1985, thus reflecting an "economy of scale" as the program's volume of clients has grown. One of the most important trends reported in Table 3.3 is the growth in the number of "alternative care days" (the number of days that would have to be added to the detention home's aggregate detention days if the home detention program did not exist). In 1982, the home detention program provided a total of 4,040 alternative care days. Between 1982 and 1985, that figure increased dramatically (216%), to a total of 12,752 days of alternative care. This increase, along with increased referrals, reflect great confidence in the program. In addition, it is clear that the program is providing significant cost benefits to the county, and this will be discussed in more detail below.

TABLE 3.3
Days of Care Provided and Costs,
Cuyahoga County Home Detention Project,
1982-1985

Year	Days of Care	Average Stay (Days)	Per Diem Cost
1982	4,040	9.9	$24.25
1983	7,161	13.0	15.34
1984	8,740	13.2	14.68
1985	12,752	16.8	13.44

TABLE 3.4
Distribution of Charges Filed, Cuyahoga County
Home Detention Project, 1983-1985

Year	Felony	Misdemeanor	Total Delinquent	Status Offenses
1983	—	—	329	220
1984	251	198	449	213
1985	282	182	464	293

Finally, as is clear from Table 3.4, referrals for delinquency charges have outnumbered referrals for status offenses, 63% to 37%.

DEFINING AND MEASURING SUCCESS

As previously noted, one of the most interesting issues associated with the evaluation of home detention programs is the definition of success. Three such definitions may be applied, and each has its advocates. The first, used by the Cuyahoga County Juvenile Court and many others, views success as remaining trouble free and available to the court. This definition would consider a case successful even if there were minor infractions of the contract and even if the youth were returned to the detention center, because the youth was still available to the court, just as if he or she had been in the detention center all along. Obviously, an arrest for an alleged new offense would be viewed as a failure. In the discussion that follows, this definition will be referred to as the "least restrictive definition."

The second, "more restrictive" definition views success as remaining out of the detention center and available to the court. Minor infractions of the contract may be tolerated, but any return to the detention center would be viewed as a failure because the juvenile did not successfully complete the program.

A third possible definition, the "most restrictive," would view as successes only those cases in which the youths remained out of the detention center and available to the court, committed no new offenses, and did not violate their contractual agreements.

Obviously, the operational definition of success has great implications in assessing the effectiveness of any program, and this one is no exception. Given available data, only the first two definitions will be discussed here. Measurement of programmatic success based on the third, "most restrictive," definition above is not feasible, since it is impossible to know how many contract violations either were unobserved or not officially reported as a result of discretion by caseworkers.

Table 3.5 indicates what the program's success rates were for 1983-1985 according to the *least restrictive* definition of success (that used by the court).

These success rates are extremely high. Furthermore, as revealed in

TABLE 3.5
Success Rates (Least Restrictive Definition),
Cuyahoga County Home Detention Project,
1983-1985

Year	Success Rate (in percentages)
1983	97.8
1984	95.2
1985	94.2

Table 3.6, there is little variance in success between preadjudicatory and postadjudicatory referrals.

In order to evaluate the success of the program according to the *more restrictive* definition (remaining out of the detention center and available to the court), a random sample (N = 417) of the client population (1981-1985) was constructed. This sample was highly representative of the program's clientele, as indicated by the descriptive summary of the sample's composition in Table 3.7.

In applying this second, more restrictive definition, the key difference is in the statistical treatment of what might be termed *in-program failures.* In the earlier analysis, using the least restrictive definition, youths who were returned to the detention home were not counted as failures because they had not been arrested for new alleged offenses and were still available to the court for their hearings. An alternative view of such cases, however, is that they do, in fact, represent program failures *if the goal is to keep the youth in the community*, rather than locked up in the detention home.

TABLE 3.6
Pre- and Postadjudicatory Success Rates
(Least Restrictive Definition), Cuyahoga
County Home Detention Project, 1983-1985

Year	Success Rates (in percentages)	
	Preadjudicatory	Postadjudicatory
1983	97.3	98.3
1984	94.5	95.8
1985	95.1	93.8

TABLE 3.7
Characteristics of Five-Year Random Sample
Cuyahoga County Home Detention Project

	Sex (percentages)	Race (percentages)	Offenses/Charges (percentages)
Male	64		
Female	36		
Black		53	
White		46	
Other		1	
Delinquency			61
Status			39
Mean number days in detention home	2.90		
Mean number home detention days	13.74		
Mean age (years)	15.13		

NOTE: N = 417.

Applying this operational definition results in lower success rates than those obtained according to the least restrictive definition. Table 3.8 presents the revised success rates for the aggregate sample and for specified client population subgroups during 1981-1985.

It is readily apparent that success rates do vary, especially by sex and by offense category. There is, in fact, an interaction effect between these two variables. That is, males constitute a far higher proportion of delinquency referrals, while females are much more likely to be referred for status offenses. In 1984, for example, 85% of all delinquency complaints filed in the Cuyahoga County Juvenile Court involved males, while 52% of all status offense referrals were females. These sex-related differences may be attributable in part to actual differences in behavior; however, they also reflect a traditional cultural belief that females need greater protection and supervision. Hence, they are subjected to intervention for more "minor" transgressions, often status offenses, whereas boys are "expected" to act out more and may have to commit a more serious violation before being subjected to official intervention.

Confidential interviews with five program staff members produced a great deal of useful information, and some of that information may help to explain the lower success rate for females and the somewhat lower rate for status offenders, a majority of whom are females. Each

TABLE 3.8
Success Rates (More Restrictive Definition)
for Five-Year Random Sample,
Cuyahoga County Home Detention Project
(in percentages)

Overall sample	82
Males	87
Females	73
Blacks	82
Whites	83
Delinquency charges	84
Status offense charges	79
Age	
11	100
12	69
13	87
14	82
15	83
16	74
17	86
18	100

NOTE: Age-specific success rates for 11- and 18-year-olds are not reliable due to insufficient subsamples in these two age categories.

interviewee was asked his or her opinion as to the most difficult cases to supervise. Here is what some of them told us:

Unruly girls. They are often in an emotional state and have environmental problems.

Unruly girls. They are ruled by hormones, not reason. They're very emotional and distrustful. Often, they've been physical/sexual abuse victims.

Unruly females. We get them at 14-15, and the pattern is already established (negative behavior, no discipline, allowed to do what they want).

Unruly girls. Their crimes tend to be more emotionally oriented. Boys commit more crimes of opportunity—they're not likely to rob you unless the opportunity presents itself [Huff, 1986].

Thus four of the five persons interviewed (including men and women and supervisory and line staff) indicated that the "toughest" youths to supervise in home detention are "unruly females." This opinion is shared by the project's director. The view that emerged from these interviews is that "unruly girls" tend to be more difficult to control because they are often involved in "emotional" and expressive behaviors, rather than instrumental acts.

At first, this observation seemed blatantly "sexist," but staff members and the director independently explained that these girls are often very dependent on boyfriends who live elsewhere and that they are anxious to leave their own homes to join their boyfriends, who frequently manipulate these girls through various promises. For example, a girl whose home environment may be unsatisfying or filled with conflict, may keep running away to join her boyfriend and may even be willing to help support her boyfriend's drug habit by prostituting herself in return for his promises of support, protection, and eventual marriage.

Program staff indicate that it is very difficult to get such girls to abide by their contractual agreements to remain at home unless authorized to leave. Status offenses, such as running away from home, school truancy, and "unruly behavior," typically involve more effectively based (emotional) motivations and may, therefore, be less amenable to rationally based deterrents, especially when status offenders are less subject to serious punishments. Even if returned to the detention home, they are less likely to receive serious punishment upon adjudication.[2]

Casework staff were also asked which cases are the easiest to supervise. Here is a sample of their responses:

> A 17-year-old who has been to DYS (the state's youth corrections authority) and has a felony charge. . . . Why? Because they've been through the system, they know the ropes, and they believe they'll be shipped away because they've already had that happen to them. They don't want to go back to DYS and be locked up. They'd rather be in the community, drinking and screwing. Their crimes are opportunistic. The reason home detention works is that we remove the opportunity. We make sure they keep their agreement and we're in school every day.

> Kids charged with felonies. Because they realize the seriousness of the charges and know they must respond positively. They're looking for help and know they must respond because they're in trouble.

> Delinquent boys. Those with low drug involvement [Huff, 1986].

Ironically, then, those whose offenses reflect more instrumental behaviors, who are more "rational" than emotional, and, often, who have a history of felony offenses and have "done time" in the state's youth corrections system may be more amenable to this type of social control. Several staff members noted that those with such backgrounds often seem to understand that house arrest is a real "break" for them and that they may be "shipped" to an institution if they "mess up." Such youths may prefer to remain in the community, having experienced some of the deprivations of institutional life. For whatever reason, staff report that such youths are easier to reason with, easier to supervise, and seem better able to understand what will happen if they break their agreement. Having experienced institutional life, the idea that they may be returned there may represent more than an abstract, empty threat.

CORRELATES OF SUCCESS:
A CLOSER LOOK

Thus far, we have considered only aggregate rates of success for certain groups and subgroups. While useful, such aggregate rates may mask important factors. A more useful analysis, from the standpoint of policymakers and program managers, is one that allows us to assess the contribution of specific variables to the overall success rates.

Using a more sophisticated form of quantitative analysis,[3] a number of variables were considered in our search for those that might be closely related to success in the program.[4] This analysis showed that only one of the variables considered, *the number of caseworker/youth contacts,* was statistically significant in determining success in the program.[5] We believe that caseworker contacts with a youth may in fact have both deterrent and socializing effects, since they provide occasions for both monitoring and counseling or advising the youth. Again, our interviews with the casework staff helped us understand the importance of these contacts. Staff responses to a number of questions about monitoring contacts reveal their skilled use of discretionary judgment:

> Phone, school visits, home visits. I like to establish face-to-face contact. You must see a youth face-to-face each day and use a combination of methods to be effective.

I like working with the child. Parents are not a direct line to the problem. It's too easy to get wrapped up in the parents and neglect the child.

I do more work with the kids. I like surprise visits. I enlist the help of other adults and the help of the school system.

I take a direct approach, one-on-one, and I'm candid. Youth want someone to talk to.

If I see there are problems and he needs more, I'll consider what time of day (he tends to have problems) and what length of time the visit should be—for example, during unsupervised times.

Different methods work best for different ages. If they're older, I give them more slack. Also according to the family structure, the offense, and whether you know the reasons for their problems.

I supervise an unsupervised child more. You generally know which kids need it more [Huff, 1986].

Other program-related variables (parent contacts, other contacts, and telephone contacts) also collectively have a positive effect, but are not individually as important as face-to-face caseworker/client contacts. These four "contact variables" are highly intercorrelated, suggesting that caseworkers who have a lot of personal contacts with youths also tend to have a high number of other "monitoring contacts" related to that same case.

It is interesting that while the relationship between the number of days spent in the detention home and program success/failure was not statistically significant, it was clearly inverse. That is, the longer a youth spent in the detention home, the less likely he or she was to succeed in the home detention program. However, we cannot say with certainty that the longer stay in detention *caused* the lower success rate. The interpretation of this finding is complicated by the possibility that some selection factors may have operated to influence the outcome. For example, it may be that the most difficult youths were those who spent more days in the detention home; if so, then their lower success rate would come not as a surprise. In any event, the overall relationship between time spent in the detention home and subsequent adjustment, as measured by success in the program, was a negative one.

PROGRAM FUNDING AND COSTS

As noted earlier, the program, initially funded via the LEAA, has become increasingly dependent on state subsidies for its operations. Table 3.9 reports the amount of state youth services subsidies awarded to the Cuyahoga County Home Detention Project for the five most recent fiscal years.

These subsidies provide funds for program staff salaries and benefits. Other costs are borne by Cuyahoga County.

As previously noted, the program provided 8,740 alternative care days (ACDs) in 1984 and increased that figure to 12,752 ACDs in 1985. To understand what this means in terms of savings to the county, one need only examine the last available full year of cost data (1984), represented in Table 3.10.

The Cuyahoga County Home Detention Project clearly represents a substantial cost savings. Moreover, even if the state subsidies were

TABLE 3.9
State Youth Services Subsidies to Cuyahoga County
Home Detention Project, Fiscal Years 1983-1987

Fiscal Year	State Subsidy ($)
1983	98,000
1984	109,919
1985	146,826
1986	204,299
1987	222,463

TABLE 3.10
One-Year Savings to County, Cuyahoga County
Home Detention Project, 1984

Alternative-care-days provided	8,740
Cost per day, detention home	$79.56
Cost per day, home detention	$14.68
Comparable cost of care, detention home	$695,354.40
Comparable cost of care, home detention	$128,303.20
One-year savings to county	$567,051.20

lost for some reason, the county would still realize a savings of several hundred thousand dollars as a direct benefit of this program.

JUDICIAL SUPPORT
FOR THE PROGRAM

The program enjoys another major benefit: the strong support from the judiciary. Based on interviews conducted with three of the five judges, the program is well regarded. The increasing referrals to the program provide another indicator of this support by the judges (and the referees, as well). This judicial support is even more impressive in light of the fact that this particular court has five judges whose judicial philosophies range from liberal to conservative, and who frequently disagree on many important issues. The program's director believes that one reason for the judiciary's confidence in the program is their awareness that the youths they refer will be closely supervised, not merely turned loose.

OTHER ISSUES:
DISCRETION AND "TURF"

While not necessarily related to program outcomes, two other issues emerged from confidential interviews with home detention project staff. The first of these issues concerns the degree of discretion exercised by the home detention staff. There was some indication that, as might be expected in any program staffed by human beings, staff members varied in their use of discretion. For example, when asked their personal philosophies about revoking home detention and returning a youth to the detention home, staff responses reflected a considerable range of "tolerance" for minor violations, as illustrated by the following two comments:

I have a strong policy. The kids are very aware of what the rules are. Any rule violation and they come back. You don't teach anything if you ignore infractions.

The degree of seriousness of the incident [is the important factor]. It may build up to the point of revocation. I also consider the population in D.H. [the detention home]. I use discretion. Another factor is if a teacher wants a kid out of school [Huff, 1986].

Some staff believe that the standards and expectations applied to youths should be more uniform. These workers argue that too much variation among workers' decision making (with respect to revocation and return to the detention home, for example) is unfair to those youths who happen to have a "strict" worker. And, since some youths are placed on home detention status more than once, these youths may be confused and even "set up" for failure if, over time, they are supervised by workers with significantly different "tolerances."

By way of contrast, other staff emphasized the importance of allowing workers the flexibility to exercise their judgment:

Home detention staff must have the latitude to make field judgments. If possible, staff should talk to the director before bringing a kid back in, but if you're out there and it's happening, you have to bring them back [Huff, 1986].

These workers argue that it would be impossible to create uniform policies to be applied to events that are inherently nonuniform. This debate is, of course, commonplace in criminal/juvenile justice administration, and each side has its advocates.

The second issue of importance concerns the possibility that home detention programs may be perceived as "competing" with probation programs, especially where more intensive probation programs exist. In addition, given the usual high caseloads of traditional probation programs, probation officers with anywhere from 30 to 100 probationers could easily view with jealousy house arrest programs with caseloads as small as five or six per worker. This issue could be very important in some courts, and could result in some self-defeating "turf battles," if not anticipated and controlled. The goals and objectives of home detention programs must be carefully articulated and contrasted with those of other programs, especially those likely to be perceived as similar.

JUVENILE HOUSE ARREST PROGRAMS:
POLICY IMPLICATIONS

Legal Issues

Controversy exists in some parts of the nation concerning the "legality" of house arrest. Objections to the use of *house arrest* are often based on the assertion that this practice is not specifically authorized by most state legislatures, since state codes, in discussing permissible placements for juveniles, usually do not use the terms *house arrest* or *home detention*. However, our research indicates that state legislatures have commonly granted juvenile court judges ample discretion to issue home detention orders. For example, in delineating permissible places of detention, Ohio's Revised Code recognizes as acceptable, "any other suitable place designated by the court" (Ohio Revised Code, 1984). Surely such language is broad enough to encompass the home (or a home) as a suitable place if so designated by the court. All that would remain, then, would be a semantic distinction between "home detention" and "conditional release" to custodial parent or guardian.

House arrest also affords a less intrusive type of control, one that corresponds more closely to the recommendations of the American Bar Association/Institute of Judicial Administration's (1980) *Standards*. Standards 6.6 and 6.7 and the accompanying commentaries are especially relevant and are reproduced in Appendix A of this report. Even the Supreme Court's controversial decision concerning the *preventive detention* of juveniles (*Schall v. Martin*, 1984) was limited to an environment where due-process protections and the conditions of confinement far exceed those typically encountered in the juvenile justice system in America (Brown, et al., 1985).

Thus it appears that house arrest is not only legally permissible, but also may be viewed as a less intrusive form of control that is consistent with the philosophy, articulated by several national commissions and many experts, that the least restrictive means available should be used as often as possible. From this perspective, the restrictive measure of secure detention should be reserved for only a small percentage of juveniles, particularly those who may pose "a clear and present danger" to the community.

Potential Effects on
Detention Population and Costs

A number of highly respected researchers have concluded that the movement toward "community based corrections," discussed in the previous chapter, has not had the results we expected, especially with respect to the number of youths held in detention facilities and other institutions (both public and private). Instead of declining, this population of detained youths has actually risen, and in some states the increase has been dramatic (Vinter et al., 1976; Rutherford and Bengur, 1976; Lerman, 1980; Center for the Study of Youth Policy, 1986).

The widespread implementation (and, where they already exist, responsible expansion) of home detention programs could significantly reduce the population of local juvenile detention centers—an effect that could greatly alleviate some of the overcrowded conditions now existing in many parts of the nation by weaning us from our dependency on secure institutions as a policy of choice in dealing with a wide array of juveniles, many of whom appear to pose no threat to public safety.

To illustrate the potential impact that a home detention program could have in a large, urban county, consider the case of Franklin County, Ohio (Columbus and its metropolitan areas).[6] Data were obtained concerning the aggregate number of juveniles slated into the Franklin County Juvenile Detention Center for 1985 and the primary charges filed against them (Alliance for Cooperative Justice, 1986). These data are presented in Table 3.11 along with estimates of the proportion in each category for whom house arrest or other options could be used as preadjudicatory alternatives.

These estimates are only preliminary, since much important case-level data are not available for consideration. No secondary analysis can substitute adequately for first-hand judicial review on a case-by-case basis, using all of the information available for each youth. Nevertheless, it should be noted that these estimates are conservative and were derived by (1) considering the seriousness and violent or nonviolent nature of the primary charge; (2) assuming (based on interviews with officials) that approximately 80% of juveniles represented in these data have either a custodial parent or guardian; (3) assuming that in certain offense categories, few or none of those represented would be considered appropriate risks for home detention

TABLE 3.11

Potential Reduction Effect of Home Detention Program (HD)
and Other Alternatives (Other) on Franklin County, Ohio,
Juvenile Detention Population, 1985

Primary Charge	N	HD	Other
Petit theft/unauthorized use	706	565	141
Burglary/B & E	350	–[b]	–
Disorderly conduct/jaywalk/indecency	302	242	60
Assault/menancing	291	–	–
Motion	258	–	–
Criminal trespass/damaging/mischief	250	140	110
Receiving stolen property	184	147	37
Felony theft	146	?	?
Traffic order-in	144	115	29
Resisting arrest/obstruct/escape	130	0	0
Curfew violation	110	88	22
Miscellaneous charges (warrants, etc.)	109	–	–
Robbery	103	0	0
Carrying concealed weapon/P.C.T.	95	0	0
Misdemeanor drug/alcohol offenses	94	75	19
Home truancy	68	0	68
Incorrigible	39	0	39
Felonious/aggravated assault	26	0	0
Rape/gross sexual imposition	24	0	0
Prostitution/soliciting/loitering	24	12	12
Status alcohol offense	20	10	10
Arson	18	0	0
School truancy	18	14	4
Forgery	14	11	3
Littering	7	5	2
Murder/vehicular homicide	5	0	0
Vandalism	4	3	1
Aggravated riot	4	0	0
Discharging weapons	3	–	–
Drug trafficking	1	0	0
Kidnapping/abduction	1	0	0
Totals	3,548[a]	1,427	557
		[HD + Other = 1,984 (56%)]	

a. Total reflects 94% of commitments reported by Court for 1985 (remaining 6% attributable to missing data for certain dates).
b. Dashes represent estimates that are not possible without detailed case-level information.

or other alternatives to detention; and (4) assuming that because of the nature of certain charges (for example, home truancy, incorrigibility), the home situation may not be amenable to home detention or the parents or guardians may be unwilling to sign a contractual agreement for home detention. In the latter circumstances, preliminary estimates assumed that other options would be more suitable than home detention and clearly superior to commitment to the detention center.

As illustrated in Table 3.11, 40% of all juveniles slated into the Franklin County Juvenile Detention Center in 1985 would appear to have been likely candidates for house arrest, as practiced by the leading programs in the United States. An additional 16% appear to have been prospects for other alternatives to detention. It should be noted that available data did not indicate the number of youths who were, in fact, placed on some type of conditional release or referred to an alternative program by the Franklin county Juvenile Court. For this reason the potential population-reduction effect cannot be measured with specificity.

Despite the caveats noted above, it is evident form this illustration, and from the information accumulated from national exemplary programs that house arrest programs have considerable potential for reducing overcrowded detention facilities, forestalling the need to construct additional facilities, and saving significant sums of money when compared to the operational costs of detention centers.

"Quality Control"

Available evaluative data (Huff, 1986) underscore the importance of "quality control" in the structure and operation of house arrest programs. Important variables include competent management and staff; good working relations between the home detention program and the juvenile court; small caseloads (five to six) for caseworkers; and emphasis on frequent contacts, including at least one unscheduled daily contact with each youth.

Public Acceptance and Support

Finally, there is the important issue of public support. Most citizens probably were unaware of house arrest programs until the recent publicity surrounding house arrest programs for adults (often focusing on programs using electronic surveillance, such as electronic "ankle bracelets"). Managers of house arrest programs must be fully cognizant of the need to develop and maintain community support, since any alternative to confinement may be viewed as a test of community tolerance. Three factors would appear to be especially important in developing and maintaining support in the community:

(1) *Careful and responsible screening of all candidates for home detention.* It would be advisable, for example, to eliminate from consideration those charged with violent, interpersonal offenses.[7] These offenses pose the greatest threat to public safety; therefore, those charged with such offenses pose the greatest potential risk to the community. House arrest programs accepting such referrals put at risk the survival of the entire program, since community backlash to one highly publicized assault could quickly undermine the program's base of political support.

(2) *Aggressive, frequent, unscheduled monitoring of all youths during their time in the house arrest program and a willingness to return them to secure detention when necessary.* Frequent contact with these youths is the most important variable associated with successful completion of home detention. *For this to occur, caseload size should not exceed five to six per worker.*

(3) *To prevent misunderstanding and to clarify expectations, all agreements should be written and should specify all conditions imposed and all expectations, as well as possible sanctions* that may be imposed if the agreement is violated. For those youths who do not comply with their agreements and whose behavior poses a risk to the public, return to secure detention should be viewed as protection of the public via crime *prevention*, and not simply categorized as a "failure."

(4) *Communication of programmatic goals and achievements to the community and to other agencies.* House arrest program managers must be acutely sensitive to the fact that such programs constitute a continuing test of community tolerance. Such programs must be operated responsibly, in the public's interest, and the public and relevant agencies must be accurately informed concerning the program's goals and achievements.

IMPLICATIONS OF HOUSE ARREST
POLICY FOR JUVENILE COURTS

The juvenile court, as a separate entity, is a comparatively recent invention, having begun in Chicago less than a century ago (1899). Juvenile courts throughout America are presently under attack by critics who charge that there is no need for a special court for juveniles and that many more youths should be confined in secure institutions. However, empirical data discussed in this chapter indicate that despite the "community corrections" movement, more, not fewer, juveniles have been confined in secure detention facilities and other institutions. Thus it would appear that the juvenile courts *have not* been "soft" on juvenile crime. Instead, much available research suggests that a large proportion of those juveniles confined in secure detention facilities, jails, and other institutions appear to pose no threat to public safety and could safely be handled via other forms of social control, including release.

It will be difficult for juvenile courts to resist the political pressure to "lock up" more young people as a way of demonstrating concern about "the crime problem." And for house arrest programs to grow, both the legislative and executive branches of local government may have to contend with another strong force: resistance from those whose jobs, funding, and power base are dependent upon our continued reliance on *institutional* corrections, rather than on community-based alternatives to confinement. If house arrest programs are successful in developing and maintaining the support of their juvenile courts and their communities, and avoiding the potential "turf battles" and structural conflicts discussed above, they can represent a less intrusive method of social control and a source of significant cost savings. Such programs, when properly structured and well managed, can be very successful in keeping juveniles "trouble-free and available to the court." The careful development and responsible expansion of such programs can have many positive effects on the administration of juvenile justice in America.

NOTES

1. Since this is the proper name of the program, the terms *house arrest* and *home detention* will be used interchangeably in this discussion and are meant to be equivalent.

2. Statewide legislation in Ohio (Amended Substitute House Bill 440) essentially precludes the commitment of status offenders to the state's youth corrections institutions.

3. Logistical regression analysis was used, with the dependent variable (outcome) being success/failure in the program.

4. These included *demographic variables* (race, age, and sex); *court-related variables* (number of detention home days, offense); and *program-related variables* (number of child contacts, number of parent contacts, number of other contacts, number of phone contacts, and number of days in program).

5. $p = < .02$.

6. These estimates were originally prepared at the request of Dr. Eugene Arnold and Franklin County Commissioner Dorothy Teater, cochairs of the Franklin County Juvenile Facility Planning Facility, to assist that committee in determining the bed-space needs for a proposed new juvenile detention facility for Franklin County, Ohio.

7. Careful screening should also take into account police reports and such factors as "overcharging" by prosecutors and "felony murder" charges, which may not accurately reflect violent behavior or intent.

4

House Arrest Programs for Adult Offenders in Kentucky and Florida

In this chapter, descriptive and analytical attention is directed to two different home incarceration programs that are used primarily with adult offenders. The first involves electronic monitoring while the second does not. Both forms of home incarceration are found in Florida, but Kentucky has only home incarceration with electronic monitoring. Before examining these programs, a general discussion of electronic monitoring will be helpful because so few people have actually witnessed its use within any criminal justice system. Our discussion includes a description of transmitter-based monitoring, active and passive monitoring, types of monitoring equipment, and the vendors who have produced or are developing monitoring equipment. We will also describe types of programs that involve the use of monitoring equipment. Then we will examine the Kentucky and Florida programs.

Until recent years, the most commonly used electronic monitoring involved equipment that did not require any interaction or communication between those conducting the monitoring and the object or person being monitored. Here we have the type of system that relies on a transmitter sending a signal that is monitored by a receiver. Such systems are often called "tracking systems" because the person or object "tracked" does not actively or deliberately interact with the receiver(s). For home incarceration programs such a system would involve an offender wearing a transmitter that would emit a signal that could be monitored by a supervising officer outside the offender's home. The signal could be sent to an officer located in a car equipped with a receiver, or the signal could be transmitted by a communications tower that would relay the signal to a central computer. The computer would receive the signal constantly and a printer could be used to create a "hard" record of a person's absence or presence in his or her home. Officers using cars equipped with a receiver would record offenders' presence or absence only when they were within the signal range of the transmitter. This system can be used when random checking on the absence or presence of an offender is desired.

When constant surveillance is preferred, a different monitoring system is used. Such an arrangement is called an "active" system; it is distinguished from the system just described because it requires a telephone to operate. As with the previous system, a transmitter is used. It is attached around an offender's ankle, wrist, or neck. The transmitter sends a signal to a receiver that is connected to the offender's telephone. Then a signal is sent to a central computer that has been specifically coded to reflect the offender's sentence. That is, the computer has been programmed to know when the offender is required to be at home or allowed to be absent for work, education, counseling, or some other approved activity.

The offender's movement is also limited by how far the transmitter can send a signal. Usually the distance is between 100 and 150 feet. Should the offender exceed this distance from the receiver, or leave home without authorization, a signal is sent to the computer and a violation is recorded. In most programs an unauthorized absence is a serious matter that may be interpreted as an "escape," which will result in traditional jail incarceration.

"Passive" systems, by comparison, do not provide constant monitoring. Rather, they are activated by a random call generated by a computer that asks that the offender verify his or her presence in the home. This may be accomplished by inserting a special wristlet transmitter into a verification box that is attached to the phone. Then a signal is sent to a computer. If the offender is unable to answer the phone, or if the phone is busy, or if an operator intercepts the call or the response, an "exception report" is recorded. Another type of passive system relies on the offender answering questions. This allows the offender's voice to be verified by a voiceprint previously programmed into a computer.

The system most frequently in use today involves an active system that relies on a small transmitter attached to the offender's ankle. In some instances the transmitter is worn around the waist; this avoids any embarrassment for offenders whose life-style or employment affords exposure of the ankle or wrist.

At the time of this writing, 12 vendors are producing monitoring equipment intended for use with criminal justice programs. These products are relatively diverse in terms of having been subjected to field tests, pilot projects, and continued efforts to improve performance. Only the monitor produced by Corrections Service, Inc., West Palm Beach, Florida, has received Federal Communications Commission approval. None of the vendor's products have "UL" approval. However, each monitor worn by an offender has one similar feature: It is relatively small and light in weight, and it is becoming smaller and more reliable (see Schmidt, 1986, p. 56 for a brief discussion of vendors and their products.)

The earliest program began in December 1984, in Palm Beach, Florida, under the guidance of Pride, Inc., a nonprofit organization. (More will be said about this program later in this chapter.) Today, more than 50 different home incarceration sites are operating in the United States. They include programs based in the state, county, or city; they are located in jurisdictions as diverse as Kenton County, Kentucky; Nassau County, New York; Lake County, Illinois; Denton County, Texas; Clackamus County, Oregon; Englewood, Colorado; Michigan's Department of Corrections; Utah's Department of Corrections, plus several other sites, with many in Florida.

These programs and others not mentioned, acquired their monitoring equipment through a variety of arrangements with vendors. These include direct purchases, leases, and lease-purchases. The costs of the equipment also vary, depending on the number of individual monitoring units needed and the quality and number of extra features of the supportive computers, receivers, and printers. In early May 1986, the average daily cost for 20 units amortized for two years, ranged from $1.76 to $9.04. The amortized unit prices drop as more units are purchased. For example, Correctional Services, Inc., West Palm Beach, Florida, quotes a purchase price of $5.26 for 20 units and $3.60 for 50 units. Regardless of the range of prices and the variety of ways to purchase equipment, it is important to remember that electronic monitoring and home incarceration are being used on a growing variety of offenders. For example, while the early program operated by Pride, Inc. was limited to drunk drivers and other traffic offenders, it now includes individuals who cannot make their bail at the pretrial stage and fathers guilty of failing to pay child support. In two instances in Florida, a federal judge sentenced counterfeiters to home incarceration with electronic monitoring. Similar variations can now be found across the United States, some of which include juvenile delinquents and persistent property offenders. While we do not have definitive information on how many offenders or exactly what type of offenders are sentenced to home incarceration with electronic monitoring, we are certain the numbers exceed 2,000 and they are rapidly growing. They include adult misdemeanants, felons, and juveniles. One of the most innovative developments, for example, permits a woman who was convicted of drunk driving in Florida to spend her sentence of home incarceration with electronic monitoring in her new residence in New Jersey by using an "800" number assigned to Pride, Inc. in Florida.

We now begin our examination of home confinement programs in Kentucky and Florida, two places where they have been employed with adult offenders. Kentucky has only one site using home incarceration and electronic monitoring, although other sites are expected to develop similar programs because the state approved enabling legislation for home confinement with electronic monitoring in its 1986 meeting of its general assembly. Florida has several different sites that rely on house arrest, and one of the programs is statewide, operated by the Florida Department of Corrections. Two special programs to be examined are located at Palm Beach County, Florida. One is operated by a nonprofit organization and the other by the county's sheriff.

THE KENTON COUNTY, KENTUCKY PROJECT

A receptive audience to home confinement and electronic monitoring was found in Kenton County, Kentucky's judge-executive and the county jailer; both were interested in complying with court injunctions to reduce jail overcrowding (*Kentucky Post*, 1984a). Between early November 1984, and late January 1985, Kenton County decided to try home incarceration with electronic monitoring devices similar to the equipment developed by Tom Moody of Tavernier, Florida, and Correctional Services, Inc., West Palm Beach, Florida.

This development followed a 1984 Kentucky General Assembly bill (Ky. H.B. 8.305), which was written to give statutory support to home incarceration with electronic monitoring. The bill was the result of more than two years of extensive groundwork including examination by interested scholars,[1] the generation of bipartisan sponsorship within the Kentucky General Assembly and the endorsements by the Kentucky F.O.P., the Mental Health Association, and numerous other civic groups. Noteworthy also was the support given the bill by the press, which endorsed the idea (*Kentucky Post*, 1984c), and provided extensive coverage of the bill while it was in committee (*Kentucky Enquirer*, 1984, 1985; *Kentucky Post*, 1984b, 1984c, 1985).

The bill was deliberately "killed" by its sponsors as a political strategy because the general assembly became embroiled in a tax reform controversy that threatened the bill's passage. Interest in the bill continued, aided by funding from the state's Department of Corrections for a pilot study (Lilly et al., 1987). At the same time, supporters for the bill sought to implement home incarceration and electronic monitoring in a manner that would not require legislative action.[2] After the pilot project, a new bill was written for the 1986 general assembly. (See Appendix I for the bill signed into law, K.R.S. 532: 200-250.) It was signed into law in April 1986.

FINDINGS[3]

The primary reason for evaluation was to "determine if home incarceration will alleviate, in a cost effective manner, overcrowding in Kenton County's jail" (Lilly, 1985: 1). The answer to this question is that home incarceration did not substantially reduce the jail's overcrowding. With only 39 people referred and approved by P.S.I. (Presentence Investigation; see Appendices J and K) for home incarceration, too few people were directed to this alternative to produce a significant change in the jail population or create a positive economic impact on the jail or county budget.

This does not mean home incarceration had no effect. In fact, 1,712 days of incarceration occurred outside of the jail through the use of home incarceration with electronic monitoring. In the words of one of the judges in Kenton County, "Any time you can save a bed-day in jail, you have done something positive for the criminal justice system." But what did 1,712 days of incarceration outside of the jail cost? This information is presented in Table 4.1.

This information indicates that $45,661 was required to incarcerate 39 people for 1,712 days outside of the jail. At a daily maintenance fee

TABLE 4.1
Home Incarceration Expenses in Kenton County

Direct costs (Kenton County)		
hardware	$ 6,987.00	
software	17,975.00	
postage	1,301.00	
phone	100.00	
computer training	680.00	
		$27,043.00
Indirect costs (Kenton County)		
15% of salary for administrative assistant (May 1985-August 1986) (Department of Corrections)	$ 6,600.00	
one-half salary for P/P officer	12,000.00	
mileage at .18 per mile	18.00	
		$18,618.00
Total		$45,661.00

of $26 per person for jail incarceration, 1,712 days would have cost $44,512.

Using the $26 rate home incarceration with electronic monitoring cost ($45,661 – $44,512 = $1,149), $1,149 more for 1,712 days than if the 39 people spent 1,712 days in jail. As Table 4.2 shows, however, this figure is misleading and it is reduced after the salaries for the administrative assistant and the probation and parole officer are removed because their salaries did not involve the use of new funds.

As Table 4.2 indicates, the total direct and indirect costs can be reduced from $45,661 to $27,068, a reduction of $18,593. By using the $26 per day figure, the 1,172 days in jail would still cost $44,512. However, the 1,712 days spent in home incarceration cost ($44,512 – $27,068 = $17,444) $17,444 less than jail time. In addition, since the beginning of the research to date, Kenton County has received more than $9,000 in supervision fees from people sentenced to home incarceration. This means that home incarceration has the potential for costing less than jail incarceration.,

For the time of the research a total of $6,167 was received from 74% of the 39 people sentenced to home incarceration. The fee structure was based on a maximum of 25% of the offender's net weekly household income. Individuals with less than $100 net income per week paid no fees.

TABLE 4.2
Direct Costs and Limited Indirect Costs Comparisons
in Kenton County

Direct costs		
hardware	$ 6,987.00	
software	17,975.00	
postage	1,301.00	
phone	100.00	
training	680.00	
		$27,043.00
Indirect costs		
mileage	25.00	25.00
Total		$27,068.00

While cost analysis is important in this evaluation, it does not represent all that should be examined. Other subjects include (1) the different expectations of the participants in the project and whether these were satisfactorily met; (2) whether home incarceration was in fact employed as an alternative to jail sentences; (3) whether the judges used home incarceration as an additional tool by which to widen the criminal justice "net" in such a way that more and more people were incarcerated in some way; (4) whether home incarceration was more, less, or relatively equal to traditional incarceration in terms of effectiveness, and (5) the extent to which the electronic monitoring equipment functioned properly. These issues are addressed in the following sections.

Expectations and Results

The Kentucky Department of Corrections had three specific objectives for home incarceration, to:

(1) protect the citizenry of the commonwealth with a minimum of financial burden on its citizens;
(2) assist the county judge-executives and jailers in their administration of jail depopulation, as well as providing an option for district court judges in their administration of justice; and
(3) assist the offenders in accepting their responsibilities to their families and the community through treatment programs, restitution, community service, job training, and employment.

The issue of citizenry protection was approached through two criteria: Did the individual sentenced to home incarceration comply with the rules established for this form of incarceration? and, Were additional crimes committed while the individual was sentenced to home incarceration? Four people did not comply with the conditions of home incarceration. However, only three of these individuals (7.7%) were revoked from the program for direct rule violations. The three individuals were returned to the Kenton County Jail. The fourth person was removed from the program because of his inability to maintain the cost of a telephone. The three individuals returned to the jail were "caught" by the monitoring equipment (see Appendix L) *and* collaborative evidence. Thus home incarceration with electronic monitoring did appear to protect the citizens. Furthermore, the 1,712 days of home incarceration placed much less financial burden on the citizens than jail incarceration would have done, with 74% of those sentenced to home incarceration actually paying fees for their supervision.

The second objective involved two aspects: (1) Assist the county judge-executive and jailers in their administration of jail depopulations, and (2) provide an option for District Court Judges in their administration of justice. In practice, the first aspect depended largely if not entirely on the second. Depopulating the jail depended upon judges employing home incarceration as a sentencing alternative. In the words of the jailer, "Home incarceration was not used enough on the front end" (i.e., not used enough as an initial sentence to depopulate the jail).

Neither, according to the jailer, was home incarceration used enough as a condition of work release out of jail, which also depended on the approval of a district judge. According to the jailer, the judges were too conservative in their use of home incarceration. Nevertheless, the jailer liked home incarceration and wished to use it as a condition of work release without the approval of a judge.

Each of the three district judges in Kenton County voiced support for the program, and each judge sentenced someone to home incarceration. However, there was very little consistency in sentencing philosophy. One judge used home incarceration as an additional option in lieu of sentencing a person to jail. In such cases, home incarceration was actively used as an alternative to some less severe sentence than jail. For this judge, the jail is the last option within the criminal justice system, thus it is not the same type of punishment as sentencing offenders to their homes.

Another judge stated he was "just not into home incarceration all that much" because he prefers giving a lot of people jail time, even if for a short time. He elaborated that it appeared to him that the probation and parole departments preferred to have individuals sentenced to home incarceration for 30 days or longer, which seemed inconsistent with the time a person would have to spend in jail of he or she were sentenced to 30 days. Because of jail overcrowding, a person sentenced to 30 days in jail would actually be out in 10 days. In addition, this judge reported that he had offered home incarceration to two individuals who refused it, saying they would rather have 10 days in jail, have the jail feed them, and pay no fees, rather than have to stay at home for 30 days, feed themselves, and pay fees. For them, 10 days in jail was a shorter and more attractive economic alternative than home incarceration with electronic monitoring.

One judge agreed with this reasoning. "As long as the jail is crowded, home incarceration cannot be tested because jail is a *good* deal," he said. (Emphasis in the original). He stated further, "If someone *needs* to be locked up, they should go to jail. Home incarceration is just not the same idea as jail incarceration." As did the jailer, this judge recommended that home incarceration with electronic monitoring continue. The other judges agreed with this recommendation.

It is clear that home incarceration with electronic monitoring did provide a sentencing option for district court judges in Kenton County. However, the judges did not seem to use home incarceration as an alternative to jail, and the option therefore had little effect as a jail depopulation objective. One judge thought of it as a "prelude" to jail, another thought of it as "not incarceration" while the other thought of it as "another" sentencing option. Thus far, home incarceration has been used conservatively in Kenton County. It has not been seriously tested as an alternative to jail incarceration.

The third major objective of the home incarceration program in Kenton County focused on assisting the offenders in accepting their responsibilities to their families and the community through treatment programs, restitution, community services, job training, and employment. The data relevant to these concerns were rather clear cut, but it is not so clear that home incarceration is responsible for the clarity. For example, 66% of those sentenced in the pilot project were employed at the time of sentencing, indicating that a sense of responsibility to oneself and family existed *prior* to the home incarceration sentence. At the same time, for example, only 16% of those in the Kenton County Jail who were employed in the work release programs. Caution must be exercised with this comparison, however, because the jail population included both misdemeanants and felons, whereas the offenders sentenced to home incarceration were all misdemeanants.

None of the offenders sentenced to home incarceration were required to engage in community services or restitution, unless payment of child support is considered restitution. If this interpretation is accepted, 3 of the 39 were involved in restitution. These three individuals represent 50% of the offenders sentenced to home incarceration because of failure to pay child support. Two of the three paid all of the back child support and maintained current child-support responsibilities. Payment of child support is interpreted as one indication of accepting responsibility, at least for these offenders.

Five of the home incarceration offenders either became involved in job training or acquired a job while on home incarceration. One male offender reported that, "Home incarceration gave me the incentive to look for work. That's the best thing that has happened to me in a long time." At the same time, eight of the offenders were required to attend Alcoholics Anonymous and did so; one person was sent to a hospital because of drug problems. If these activities are considered indicators of accepting responsibility, it can be concluded that the individuals sentenced to home incarceration tended to meet the Department of Corrections' objective that offenders accept their responsibilities to their families and communities. Additional use of community service or restitution conditions would have contributed even further to meeting this objective.

Each offender sentenced to home incarceration *could* have been sent to jail, but was not. This suggests that home incarceration may have been used as an alternative to jail. But such a sentence does not mean that the offender *would* have been sent to jail if home incarceration had not been available as an alternative. To answer this question the judges were asked if they would have sentenced the offender(s) to jail. One judge indicated that it would depend on whether the jail had any space; another judge said "half of the time, yes, and half of the time, no." The third judge indicated that, "except for the offenders who had jobs," all of those sentenced to home incarceration would have probably gone to jail.

Home incarceration does not appear to have "widened the net" in Kenton County. With only 39 people sentenced to home incarceration

TABLE 4.3
Prior Jail Time by Gender
for Total N in Kenton County

	Male		Female		Total	
	N	%	N	%	N	%
Yes	30	77.0	1	2.5	31	79.5
No	5	12.8	3	7.6	8	20.4
Total					39	100%

over a 15-month period, it would be difficult to conclude that many offenders who previously had been treated lightly were now being incarcerated at home. At the same time, it may be concluded that home incarceration was at least occasionally used as an alternative to jail, depending upon circumstances such as whether the offender happened to be employed.

As Table 4.3 shows, an examination of the records of offenders sentenced to home incarceration indicated that approximately 80% of them had received prior jail sentences. Additional data examined showed that almost 96% of the people sentenced to home incarceration had prior convictions in Kentucky. Only one person, a male, had no prior convictions. It can be concluded that home incarceration with electronic monitoring was not employed to "spread the criminal justice net," at least not to draw first offenders into the system.

Is home incarceration better than, worse than, or relatively equal to traditional incarceration in terms of effectiveness? One way to judge this is to examine recidivism. A "control group" made up of those 1984 Kenton County offenders matched with the group sentenced to home incarceration by age, gender, and prior offenses showed a 20% recidivism rate. This provides a very rough benchmark.

At this time, two of the offenders sentenced to home incarceration have been charged and convicted with new offenses. First, a woman originally charged with DUI and sentenced to 56 days of home incarceration has been convicted of the same offense. Second, an offender serving a home incarceration sentence for driving with a suspended license in Kentucky has been convicted of the same offense; he was caught driving in Kentucky with an Ohio license. Based on these cases, the recidivism rate for the Kenton County program is 5.1%.

This may mean that home incarceration is more effective than jail,

TABLE 4.4

Home Incarceration with Electronic Monitoring,
Average Days Sentenced by Offense and Gender
for Kenton County

	Male	Female
Criminal mischief	33	
DUI	49	43
Escape/work release	180	
Nonsupport	39	
Operating on suspended license	33	
Contributing to delinquency	28	
Possession of LSD		35
Attempted burglary	28	
P.I.	30	

but extreme caution is required here because of the low number of cases. In addition, we suspect that the original DUI charge for the woman and her home incarceration sentence may have been the result of preferential treatment because of her connections with employees within the criminal justice system. *Any* comparisons based upon her case are questionable. It must be concluded that the effectiveness of home incarceration with electronic monitoring, at least in terms of reducing recidivism, cannot be determined at this time.

Average length of home incarceration sentences is shown in Table 4.4. We note that the length of the sentence does not always match days actually served, although this is usually the case. Exceptions are found in those instances where an individual sentenced to home incarceration was unable to comply with the sentence because he did not have the money to pay phone bills and where an individual was sentenced to 30 days because of nonsupport but released after paying off this obligation and court costs.

A comparison between the days sentenced to home incarceration and the days an individual would have spent in jail suggested that the judges in Kenton County expected the home incarceration sentence to be approximately one-third of the traditional jail sentence. For example, a person sentenced to 5 months in jail on a revoked driving license was sentenced to 56 days of home incarceration. An offender sentenced to jail for 90 days for driving on a suspended license received 28 days of home incarceration. Of course, this is roughly equal to the jail sentence that actually would have been served because of overcrowding.

Did the electronic equipment work? The history of the electronic monitoring equipment used in Kenton County is itself an important topic that cannot be fully discussed here. One problem is that some of the equipment is already outdated because of recent technological developments spurred on by competition in the market place and the desire on the part of consumers to have fail-safe monitoring devices. These developments were expected and should be kept in mind when discussing the future of electronic monitoring. In general, however, it can be concluded that the equipment in Kenton County worked well enough for the type of offenders sentenced to home incarceration.

The equipment had several troublesome problems. First, about half of the equipment sent to Kenton County within the first two months of the project had to be returned to the manufacturer because it malfunctioned. This was a very frustrating problem to everyone involved with the project, including those sentenced to home incarceration, because they often had to return the equipment. This caused interruptions in work schedules, additional transportation costs, and anxiety as to whether the project would fail because of technological obstacles.

Furthermore, the early computer printouts on offenders were often so garbled that it became necessary in some instances to call offenders at home to see if they were present. The current equipment is much better than the original equipment; fewer equipment-based problems occur than in the past.

The staff responsible for interpreting the computer printouts has become more knowledgeable because of training and experience. They are now able to distinguish between a real violation and what appears to be a violation that in fact may be caused by a "sleeping pattern" or "dead spot" in the offender's home. The equipment may give a signal that appears as if it is a violation when in fact the offender is in his or her home perhaps asleep but with one leg on top of the other, thus preventing the transmission of a clear signal.

The acid test for the equipment is whether it picks up real violations. Our study concluded that the equipment generally did so. Three individuals were returned to jail because the equipment "caught" them. In each case, however, collaborative evidence of violation was obtained.

THE STATEWIDE FLORIDA PROJECT

Florida's Department of Corrections' interest in house arrest grew out of the need to address the state's prison overcrowding. In May 1983, a group of criminal justice officials developed the concept of "community control," which includes confinement to an offender's residence as an alternative to traditional incarceration. Offenders in the program are called "controlees." The concept was formalized in the Florida Correctional Reform Act of 1983 that provided for "a safe, diversionary alternative to imprisonment and to help address the problem of increasing prison population and associated high costs" (Flynn, 1986: 64). The Florida statutes are clear about that state's approach to home confinement:

> Community control means a form of intensive supervised custody, including surveillance on weekends and holidays, administered by officers with restricted caseloads. Community control is an individualized program in which the freedom of an offender is restricted within the community, home, or noninstitutional residential placement and specific sanctions are imposed and enforced [FS 948: 001].

Controlees are kept under close surveillance with the help of community control officers who work irregular hours, including nights, weekends, and holidays. Their task is to ensure that offenders are in their homes except when engaging in paid employment or performing approved community service work. Unlike some home confinement programs, Florida's program had the benefit of effective planning as to how the program was to be implemented. An implementation manual was developed, and it has been used to ensure statewide uniformity in program implementation. In addition, community control officers received training that addressed the new program goals. The training included self-defense, surveillance techniques, search and seizure, legality, identification of behavior disorders in mental illness, cross-cultural differences, and how to handle intensive relationships (Flynn, 1986: 66).

Florida's new statewide program, as the one in Kentucky, had the benefit of extensive positive media coverage. This was partly the result of deliberately opening the program to media scrutiny at the outset, as well as a public willingness to give the program a chance.

Unlike Kentucky's program, Florida's community control program

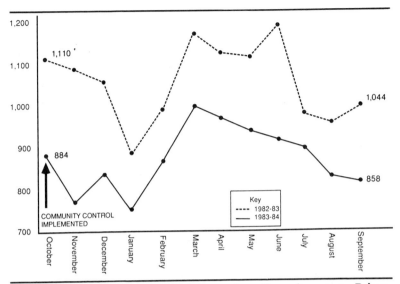

Figure 4.1   Florida Department of Corrections Commitments to Prison, October 1982-December 1984.

was explicitly grounded in a correctional philosophy. It contends that community control is a form of punishment designed to develop a controlee's accountability and responsibility. The philosophy adheres to the idea that punishment and reward are integral to "the backbone of democracy" and applicable to criminal offenders. The community control program therefore stresses self-improvement, the work ethic, and the desire on the part of offenders to want better jobs and better pay (Flynn, 1986: 64). As Leonard E. Flynn, director of probation and parole for the Florida Department of Corrections said, "These philosophical concepts are the basis of community control" (Flynn, 1986: 66). In addition, the program requires free labor for public service projects; approximately 10,000 hours of public service is contributed each month from the controlees.

In keeping with the program's emphasis on the work ethic, controlees pay monthly fees of $30-$50 to the state to offset the costs of supervision, pay restitution, and provide for their own support. Sometimes they are also required to maintain contact with their victims, neighbors, friends, creditors, and others.

How well is the program working? In terms of the major goal of reducing prison overcrowding, Figure 4.1 indicates a positive impact.

With approximately 10,000 offenders sentenced to the program since October 31, 1983, the number of prison commitments has dropped by an average of 180 per month, which is significant. Of the approximately 10,000 offenders in the program, 1,508 had their home confinement revoked; they were sent to prison. Including both technical violations and new offenses, the program has a 16.2 failure rate (Flynn, 1986: 68). An average of 300 new offenders are accepted into the program per month.

Approximately 70.3% of the controlees are described by Flynn (1986: 68) as "bona fide prison diversions"; approximately 15% are county jail diversions. These findings have been interpreted as representing positive results, especially in view of the fact it costs only $2.85 per day to supervise a community controlee compared to $27.64 per day for imprisonment.

As in Kentucky, sentencing judges are not in agreement about the program. Some judges think the length of community control terms are too long, with an upper limit of two years. Other judges think the sentences are not long enough (Flynn, 1986: 68). Generally, the objection to two-year sentences is that even a very disciplined person could not abide by the conditions of the sentences for such a length of time. Unfortunately, we do not have information about the average length of sentences served.

THE PALM BEACH COUNTY, FLORIDA PROJECTS

Two additional home confinement programs have been implemented in Palm Beach County, Florida. One is operated by Pride, Inc., a nonprofit organization, and the other is operated by the county sheriff's office. We will examine both programs. Participation in each program is voluntary.

For the last 15 years Pride, Inc. has supervised and administered misdemeanor and criminal traffic and pretrial intervention for Palm Beach County. They also operate a DWI school and a substance abuse education program. In recent years, Pride, Inc. has expanded, and they now have a total of four offices in Florida. They have more than 50 employees and an annual budget of approximately $2 million. Their interest in home confinement and electronic monitoring developed as an extension of their charge as a private supervisory agency for misdemeanant probationers and parolees. Their programs are fee based with no funds coming from the state.

Encouraged by news reports that electronic monitoring and house confinement was being used on an experimental basis in Albuquerque, New Mexico (Niederberger, 1984; Niederberger and Wagner, 1985), Judge J. Allison DeFoor, Monroe County, Florida, sentenced four people to house arrest with electronic monitoring equipment developed by Omni Communications, Inc., Tavernier, Florida. Pride, Inc. was the supervising agency for the first house arrest probationers with electronic monitors.

Shortly after the first people were sentenced to the Monroe County experimental program in late 1983, Pride, Inc.'s director of programs, Glen I. Rothbart, addressed the idea of developing a similar program in Palm Beach County, where jail overcrowding was (and still is) a serious problem. With more than 720 presentenced detainees waiting for space in other facilities, Rothbart's proposal was well received by the judicial community, especially Judge Edward ("Fast Eddie") Garrison. By late November 1984, the first offender was sentenced in Palm Beach County to house arrest with electronic monitoring. The press quickly endorsed the experiment ([Palm Beach] *Evening Times,* November 29, 1984). Since the program's inception, 144 people have been sentenced to the new alternative with Pride, Inc. as the supervising agency, of whom 124 were males. Almost all of the probationers are white (95%), and most of them were blue-collar construction workers. Very few had college educations. The 144 probationers had experienced a total of 5,900 days of incarceration outside of the jail. All were sentenced for either DWI or driving with a suspended license.

Each person on probation is expected to pay a $20 supervisory fee, plus $7 per day for electronic monitoring. Thus far, 98.3% of Pride, Inc.'s clients have paid fees of $41,000. They can also be required to pay restitution and do public service work. As an example, approximately 9% of the blood collected for medical purposes in Palm Beach County comes from people sentenced to community service. Apparently, according to Judge Garrison, community service contributions must first be approved by the sentencing judge.

Based on a $26 per day cost of jailing, the total of 5,900 days of home incarceration served from November 1984 to September 1986 represented a savings of $153,000 for Palm Beach County. Unlike the

program in Kenton County, Kentucky, the Palm Beach County
program did not require a capital investment for the monitoring
devices; nor were new funds required for additional probation and
parole officers. The only complaint, as reported by Judge Garrison, is
that not enough electronic devices are available to have a major
impact on the jail overcrowding problem.

Nevertheless, the program is considered a success; fewer than 10%
have committed new offenses since their release from the program.
With 96.8% of the probationers having had prior convictions on
charges ranging from public intoxication to second degree murder, it
appears that the program did not involve "widening the criminal
justice net." Most (73.3%) of the prior offenses related to drunken
driving. Only eight (5.5%) of the probationers were "revoked" from
home confinement because of violating the conditions of the program. Two of the violators were white women. The others included
one black man and five white men.

The Palm Beach County Sheriff's Office became involved in
December 1984 with a pilot project that eventually led to the
development of the "In-House Work Release Program." The program
was initiated by Judge Edward Garrison in cooperation with Sheriff
Richard P. Wille. Both officials were interested in reducing overcrowding at the Stockade, a facility under the administration of the
Sheriff and the county's jail system. With the Stockade overcrowded
with 352 felons, and the county planning to increase the population
to 750, an alternative form of incarceration was badly needed.[4]

Unlike the programs sponsored by Kentucky, Florida's statewide
"custody program," or Pride, Inc.'s supervisory system, the Palm
Beach County program was developed for an incarcerated population,
most of whom were felons. It followed the same statutory guidelines
(FS 9481; FS 921.187; FS 921.231; FS 948.10 and FS 948.90) created for
the statewide system of community control. In the Stockade division
only those inmates in the work release program were eligible to be
considered for "in-house arrest." Inmates convicted of murder, rape,
child molestation, armed robbery, drug charges, and vehicular
homicide were not eligible. Those seeking admission to the program
also were required to have served a large portion of their sentence,
which by statute could not exceed one year.

Of the approximately 350 inmates in the Stockade during the time
of the research, approximately 40 were always available for work
release; between 12 and 17 of the inmates in work release participated

in the In-House Arrest Work Release Program. A total of 87 offenders participated in the program between December 14, 1984 and December 31, 1985; 85 volunteered and 2 were pretrial offenders ordered by the court to participate.[5] Eligibility also required that each inmate have a good record, a residence in Palm Beach County, and a telephone. A sponsor (wife, friend, spouse, or parent) was considered desirable, but not mandatory. The participants also paid $9 per diem and they were required to return to the Stockade once a week for the equipment to be inspected.[6]

The sex composition of the program participants was 80 (92%) male, 7 (8%) female. Racially, only 10 (12.5%) of the men were black, while 64 (82%) were white; 5 (6.3%) "others" comprised the remaining males. For the women, 3 (43%) were white, 3 (43%) were black, and 1 (14.3%) was "other."

Altogether, the 87 participants accumulated 4,816 days of work release through in-house arrest and electronic monitoring. The average sentence was 55 days. According to a report on the program (Garcia, 1986), one inmate successfully completed 311 days under house arrest; 14 others completed more than 100 days. But how well did the program work?

Stockade's division commander, Lt. Eugene Garcia, strongly endorsed the program in his written report and in interviews with one of the authors.[7] For example, he stated in his final report on the program: "This concept that is beginning to sweep the nation, beyond all doubt, is the greatest thing to happen to the American taxpayer in memory" (Garcia, 1986). His assistant, Art Davis, expressed the same sentiment. He said: "This idea is the greatest thing that ever happened to the taxpayer. One man will have paid for three units by the time he leaves."[8] Unfortunately, Garcia's evaluation did not include systematic interviews with the inmates. Anecdotal reports, however, indicate that the participants "love it." The economic data presents a more complete analysis of the program's "success."

As shown in Table 4.5, by January 1, 1986, the hardware and software for the program had produced an 87% return. With 4,765 days of in-house arrest at a per diem of $9, $42,885 of revenue had been generated. Garcia predicted the investment would be making a profit by March 1, 1986, and indeed it did.

Furthermore, Garcia reported that only 3 inmates created serious problems; 1 escaped and 2 were arrested on new charges while in the

TABLE 4.5
Financial Data on Home Confinement

Hardware and software		
1 software package	$ 3,500	
computer, w/ disk drive, printer,		
screen, and communications panel	10,000	
45 receiver/dialers and transmitters at $795	35,775	
Total		$49,275
Payback (January 19, 1986)		
daily per diem	$ 9	
total days	4,765	
Total payback ($9 × 4,765)		$42,885
Percentage of return on investment		87%

SOURCE: Adapted from Garcia (1986).

program. However, of the 87 inmates who participated, only 61 were "released after successfully completing their sentences" (Garcia, 1986: 5). The others, not counting the 3 "serious problems," were removed because of general problems indicative of all work release programs such as loss of work and loss of transportation. However, a few participants were revoked because of problems at home. For example, one young man's mother had a live-in boyfriend who "set the boy up to get into trouble."[9] He was returned to the Stockade.

DISCUSSION

Each project was methodologically flawed. In addition to the small Ns in the Kentucky, Pride, Inc., and Stockade projects, the generalizability of the findings were severely limited because the individuals in the programs were not sentenced randomly. In each instance they were selected on the basis of each judge's sentencing philosophy or the approval of some other official. This limitation thus renders any definitive comparisons impossible. Other limitations include the limited time span of the projects. More serious, however, is the fact that most of the studies omitted basic information such as the socioeconomic characteristics of the people sentenced to home confinement. This raises the question of who is being permitted to experience home confinement. From our observations, it appears that most people selected from social and economic circumstances that would pretty well guarantee (1) a successful experience from them, and (2) a profitable one for the sponsoring agency. Thus far, however, none of the programs have caused a reduction in jail or prison budgets.

Other problems associated with home confinement and electronic monitoring involve criminal justice personnel. No research, for instance, has addressed the question of the potential impact of home incarceration, with or without electronic monitoring, on the status and role of probation and parole officers. In other words, are these professionals going to see their relationship to offenders change from being helping agents to surveillance agents? Furthermore, there is practically no information on the impact of home confinement and electronic monitoring on the community or the inmate's family. Nor do we have sufficient research on the reliability of the electronic monitoring equipment.

Nonetheless, the projects generated valuable results. They offered an opportunity for examining many of the ideas we have proposed regarding the potential for home incarceration with electronic monitoring and they have contributed immeasurably to writing appropriate guidelines. However, there are issues that need to be considered other than appropriate guidelines. For example, while we and others have expressed concern about how home incarceration's potential for turning every home into a prison might develop, little evidence until now has been available on this issue. Our limited research suggests this has not yet occurred given the restrained sentencing policies of the judges. We note that those people sentenced to home incarceration have tended for the most part to have prior convictions and are not "first timers." Of course, the existence of prior convictions and sentences does not *ensure* that they would have been jailed in the absence of home incarceration and electronic monitoring.

Nor do we know if the judges *would* have used home incarceration with first-time offenders who could possibly have gone to jail because these offenders seldom appear before judges for sentencing. These cases can often be handled with some form of diversion, including restitution; community service; no-contest pleas; "contracts," which state that the charge will be used against the offenders should they commit another similar offense; mediation; alternative placements in treatment centers; and conditional discharge.

We are somewhat encouraged by this development because it allays some of our fears that home incarceration with electronic monitoring would become a Trojan horse for an increasingly "carceral society" (See Foucault, 1977; Ball and Lilly, 1987). Our worst fears have yet to become reality, thus extending our hope that a totally disciplined society will be avoided. Nonetheless, we strongly recommend the use of specific guidelines as a means of reducing any such tendency. It is also important that more definitive research into "net widening" be undertaken as soon as "house arrest" has become more commonplace.

NOTES

1. See Ball and Lilly (1983a; 1983b; 1985; 1986a; 1986b; 1987) and Lilly and Ball (1987) for discussion of the scholarly interest.

2. See Ball and Lilly (1984a and 1984b).

3. Data for the pilot project was collected between May 1, 1985 and October 31, 1985; however, only 23 people were sentenced to home incarceration during this time. Since then, 16 additional offenders have been sentenced to home incarceration. We have included these in our analysis.

4. The following section relies upon a report prepared by Lt. Eugene D. Garcia, division commander of the Stockade. Supplemental information was provided to the authors on request. We are thankful and indebted to Lt. Garcia.

5. The two court-ordered participants were female AIDS victims who were removed from the jail because of fear that their lives were endangered by other inmates.

6. The program sponsored by Kenton County, Kentucky, and Pride, Inc. have the same weekly requirement.

7. Lilly, Field Notes. October 1985.

8. Lilly, Field Notes, October 1985.

9. Lilly, Field Notes, October 1985.

5

Legal and Social Issues
of House Arrest

It should be apparent at this point, that any movement toward the increased use of home confinement as an alternative to institutional detention or incarceration must confront both legal and social issues of considerable complexity. It is important that these be faced and considered. The more specific legal issues are better addressed elsewhere in consideration of examples of the use of home confinement under a variety of conditions. Here we will deal with the more general issues. The social issues tend to be even broader than the purely legal issues, placing them in a larger context. The crux of both sets of issues surrounding home confinement seems to lie in the distinction between the realms of the "public" and "private."

Of course, the relevance of some of the issues to be raised will vary enormously depending upon the particular nature of the home confinement one has in mind. Confining a 12-year-old to his or her home during certain parts of the day as an alternative to confinement in a secure detention facility is very different from placing a hardened parolee in home confinement. Monitoring of compliance by telephone or announced visits is not the same as attaching an electronic bracelet to the body of the offender. Aside form these obvious differences, the specific conditions imposed as part of the home confinement can vary greatly. This is in fact one of the strengths of this alternative. On the other hand, it makes it much more difficult to generalize about the legal and social issues. A particular issue may seem of burning relevance in one case and ridiculous to raise in another.

GENERAL LEGAL ISSUES

The tradition of house arrest has earned something of a bad
reputation because of its use in many countries as a means of
silencing political dissent. It accomplishes this not by "punishing"
the dissident with flogging or prison but merely by forcing him or her
out of the public arena and into a completely private life. As such, it is
a technique for interfering with free speech and assembly, both of
which are explicitly protected by the First Amendment to the U.S.
Constitution. Where confinement to the home might well represent a
violation of First Amendment rights, the actual monitoring of
compliance by telephone, visit, or electronic monitoring might pose
dangers to protections against "unreasonable search and seizure" as
set forth in the Fourth Amendment.

Much has changed in the past 200 years. The issue of privacy has
become more and more important as the population, which was once
rural, has become more tightly crowded together, and as once
unthinkable technological powers have emerged. When the Constitution was drafted and the Bill of Rights added, communication was
limited to face-to-face contact, letters, and print media such as
newspapers, pamphlets, and books. Physical surveillance was limited
to what could be discovered through the use of eyes and ears. Self-
incrimination was a matter of torture or otherwise forced testimony.
In general, invasions of privacy required some form of physical
trespass, interference with private property such as correspondence,
or physical coercion. Concerns over privacy go back for centuries, but
population concentration has made it more difficult to protect
privacy while technological developments have made it much easier
to invade privacy. Thus it must be considered a pressing issue.

Fourth Amendment

Any consideration of constitutional issues with respect to home
confinement is likely to focus most of its attention on possible
violations of the Fourth Amendment, which reads as follows:

The right of the people to be secure in their persons, houses, papers,
and effects, against unreasonable searches and seizures, shall not be

violated, and no warrants shall issue but upon probable cause, supported by oath or affirmation, and particularly describing the place to be searched, and the persons or things to be seized.

From its earliest days, the Fourth Amendment has been regarded as of crucial importance in maintaining the boundary between the public and private spheres. Justice Story called the clause protecting against unreasonable searches and seizures "indispensable to the full enjoyment of the rights of personal security, personal liberty, and private property" (quoted in Westin, 1967: 332). Francis Leiber wrote that the Fourth Amendment told each citizen, "Be a man—thou shall be sovereign in thy house," while expressing the "direct antagonism" of Anglo-American law to "police government" (quoted in Westin, 1967: 332). Yet in the first major case involving electronic surveillance of a private individual, *Olmstead v. United States* (1928), the Supreme Court held that a wiretap executed without an accompanying trespass in an individual's home was not a violation of the Fourth Amendment. In the *Olmstead* case, a five-to-four majority of the Court upheld the use of surreptitious wiretapping on the telephone of a bootlegger on grounds that the lines were not protected under the Fourth Amendment restrictions on search and seizure or under Fifth Amendment restrictions against self-incrimination, ruling, in effect, that the telephone lines were public and that the defendants had used them voluntarily.

Even when there was continued physical trespass onto private property during the course of electronic surveillance the Supreme Court held that individuals had no Fourth Amendment protection in state courts. Thus in the case of *Irvine v. California* (1954), evidence gained as a result of physical intrusion was held admissible in state court despite the fact that state agents entered private premises repeatedly and surreptitiously several times during the surveillance in order to plant, adjust, and finally remove a listening device placed in the defendant's bedroom so as to listen to conversation between him and his wife and monitor their telephone calls. The court would occasionally exhort the states to abide by the Fourth Amendment, but the occasional suggestions were not backed up with effective sanctions (Dionisopoulos and Ducat, 1976). Indeed, Fourth Amendment principles did not become applicable to the states in a strict way until they were enforced in *Mapp v. Ohio* (1961).

Fourteen years after the *Olmstead* decision, the Supreme Court

held that the principles governing *Olmstead* wiretapping also
governed eavesdropping. The case, *Goldman v. United States* (1942),
involved a situation in which government agents introduced evidence
gained from overhearing an incriminating conversation through use
of a sensitive microphone placed on the wall of an office adjoining
that in which the conversation took place. The Court ruled that there
had been no violation of the Fourth Amendment in that no actual
physical trespass had occurred because the agents never entered the
office under electronic surveillance. In *Silverman v. United States*
(1961), however, the District of Columbia police had monitored
conversations within the defendant's home by driving a "spike mike"
through the wall separating the home from an adjoining dwelling
and into the heating duct of the Silverman residence. The Court ruled
the evidence inadmissible in view of the fact that the domestic
boundary had been physically penetrated in this case.

In 1965 the Supreme Court took a major step toward the
enunciation of a new constitutional doctrine of privacy (Westin,
1967). In the case of *Griswold v. Connecticut* (1965) the Court
overturned a Connecticut law forbidding the dissemination of birth
control information even to married couples. The Court cited not
only the Fourth Amendment but also the First, Third, Fifth, and
Ninth Amendments as protecting a right of privacy between husband
and wife—a right even older even than the Bill of Rights. What is
especially interesting about *Griswold* is the fact that nearly every
Supreme Court justice cited a different set of constitutional guarantees
by the state of Connecticut.

Most directly related to the Fourth Amendment, however, is the
landmark case of *Katz v. United States* (1967), which came only two
years after the *Griswold* decision. In the *Katz* case government agents
attached a monitoring device to the outside of a public telephone
booth and recorded the defendant's conversation without his knowl-
edge or consent. Overruling *Olmstead* and *Goldman*, the Court held
that the absence of a physical trespass into the telephone booth, even
in a public setting, did not justify a violation of the defendant's
reasonable expectation of privacy. This decision is especially noteworthy in that it represented a new conception of privacy that had less
to do with the breach of a boundary between a public space and a
private property space than with an intrusion upon *personal* privacy.
Indeed, the Court went so far as to say that "the Fourth Amendment
protects people, not places" (*Katz*, 1967: 351).

Judicial decisions following *Katz* made determination as to whether an illegal "search and seizure" has taken place dependent upon whether or not a "reasonable expectation of privacy" was violated. The Supreme Court has relied upon a two-part formulation combining both subjective and objective tests in determining whether there was a "reasonable expectation of privacy" in a given case, developed in Justice Harlan's concurring opinion in Katz as follows:

> first that a person have exhibited an actual expectation of privacy and, second, that the expectation be one that society is prepared to recognize as "reasonable" [*Katz*, 1967: 361].

The subjective aspect of the test stresses the extent to which the individual has "exhibited" an expectation of privacy by taking actions to *protect* that privacy. This would include such actions as closing the door of a telephone booth, closing the door of a room, moving away from others present in a particular area, and closing blinds or curtains. The subjective aspect of the test also involves the extent to which the individual assumes risks that might *reduce* any expectation of privacy, such as by revealing information to another. In *United States v. White* (1971), for example, a case in which an informer consented to wear a hidden microphone and have his conversations with the defendant recorded, the Court held that no Fourth Amendment violation had occurred. The Court ruled that a defendant does not have a "justifiable and constitutionally protected expectation that a person with whom he is conversing will not then or later reveal the conversation to the police" (*U.S. v. White*, 1971: 749). The Court reasoned that because there was no reasonable expectation of privacy in such situations in the first place, the use of an electronic device to listen to and record the conversation could not be construed as a violation of Fourth Amendment protections. Criticisms of the *White* decision focused on the impression that the Court seemed to be saying that every friend and acquaintance should be assumed to be a potential informer.

The objective aspect of the *Katz* test as to whether the individual has a reasonable expectation of privacy rests upon a community standards notion as to what society might be expected to regard as a "reasonable expectation" under the circumstances. Part of the problem here is that no objective referent is specified; the term *society* is left undefined (Office of Technology Assessment, 1985). Does *society* refer to recent opinion polls, social traditions, the concept of the reasonable person, or to something else entirely? In practice the Court seems to have constructed a continuum ranging from the traditionally closed private spaces in which all possible boundaries are erected so as to separate this realm from the public realm to the completely open, purely public sphere. Thus there would be a clearly reasonable expectation of privacy in a situation in which the individual went inside his or her own home, locked the doors, closed the windows and curtains, and turned off the lights, thus establishing almost every possible boundary. At the other end of the continuum where an individual might be standing in the middle of a playing field in a stadium filled with thousands of legitimate spectators, there clearly would be no reasonable expectation of privacy at all.

In recent years the Court had modified the objective test with references to a "legitimate" rather than a "reasonable" expectation of privacy. Thus in the more recent case of *Rakas v. Illinois* (1978) the Court refers to expectations of privacy "which the law recognizes as 'legitimate'" (quoted in Office of Technology Assessment, 1985: 17). Under this doctrine the courts would not ask if society might regard an expectation of privacy in a certain situation as reasonable but would turn to the law itself to see what the law had recognized as a "legitimate" expectation. This had the advantage of providing a less subjective definition, but it seems to assume that the laws to be examined are correct and need not be evaluated against more fundamental principles such as those contained in the Fourth Amendment (Office of Technology Assessment, 1985).

In *Berger v. New York* (1967), the Supreme Court dealt specifically with the constitutional requirements for a wiretap (del Carmen, 1982). The Supreme Court held in this case that the language of a statute authorizing wiretapping was too broad and therefore in violation of rights protected by both the Fourth and the Fourteenth Amendments. The Court indicated that a valid warrant authorizing any form of electronic surveillance must satisfy six basic requirements. These include requirements that (1) the warrant describe in particular the conversations that are to be overheard, (2) probable cause to believe that a specific crime has been or is being committed must be shown, (3) the surveillance must be for a limited period of time, (4) the suspects whose conversations are to be overheard must be named, (5) a return of the warrant must be made to the court showing what conversations were intercepted, and (6) the surveillance must cease when the specific information sought has been obtained. The *Berger* decision specified the constitutional requirements for electronic surveillance, and states have since complied with these requirements by statute or court decisions (del Carmen and Vaughn, 1986).

In 1977 the Supreme Court directly addressed the question of governmental surveillance by pen registers that can be attached at the telephone company offices to record the telephone numbers dialed from a particular telephone (del Carmen, 1982). Acting in this case, *United States v. New York Telephone Company* (1977), the Court ruled that pen registers were acceptable because they simply record numbers dialed from a given telephone and do not actually intercept conversations. In *Smith v. Maryland* (1979), which was decided two years later, the Court confronted the issue of whether the pen registers represented a violation of the "search and seizure" restrictions of the Fourth Amendment. According to the Court, the use of a pen register located at the offices of the telephone company did not constitute a violation of the Fourth Amendment in that there was no legitimate expectation of privacy in such a situation.

Two more recent cases focused upon the use of "beepers" that can be attached to objects or individuals, which emits a signal that allows for the tracing of movements. In *United States v. Knotts* (1983) the Supreme Court ruled that the monitoring of a beeper without a warrant was not a search or seizure under the Fourth Amendment because there was no reasonable expectation of privacy in that the movements being tracked were public movements. The *Knotts* case involved the installation of a beeper in a container of chloroform, with the consent of the seller, which was then bought by the defendant for use in a drug manufacturing operation. The beeper assisted in visual surveillance as the defendant moved along public roads, thus enabling law enforcement offices to trace the container to a private dwelling, a cabin used by the defendant.

The *Knotts* case is especially interesting because it highlights the distinction between the *installation* of an electronic surveillance device and subsequent *monitoring* employing the service. In this case the Court ruling applied only to the monitoring issue, although the installation itself had also taken place without a warrant. The court was not forced to rule on the actual installation of the device in that the defendant acknowledged a lack of legal standing to make a challenge. In the cases of *United States v. Miroyan* (1978) and *United*

States v. Bruneau (1979), lower courts had acknowledged that the initial installation of a beeper could represent a potential violation of the Fourth Amendment. In both cases, however, the courts concluded that Fourth Amendment rights were not violated when it was clearly established that the device was installed with the express consent of the owner of the conveyance in question and while that vehicle was within his total dominion.

In *United States v. Karo* (1984), a decision coming one year after the *Knotts* decision, the Supreme Court addressed two major issues not faced in *Knotts*. The first of these had to do with the question of whether the installation per se of a beeper into a container of chemicals constituted a violation of Fourth Amendment restrictions with respect to search and seizure. The second issue had to do with whether or not the subsequent monitoring after the container had been taken into a private residence not available to visual surveillance represented a violation of Fourth Amendment protections. It may be useful to examine each of these issues in turn.

In the *Karo* case an informer had provided information that the defendants had ordered a supply of ether to be used in the production of cocaine. Law enforcement officers installed a beeper in one of the containers that was later sold to the defendants. The movement of this container was monitored for months, after which a warrant was obtained allowing for a search of the residence of one of the defendants. Ruling on the question of the installation of the beeper in the first place, the Court held that it represented no violation of the Fourth Amendment because the installation had been made with the consent of the seller, who was the full owner of the property at the time. The private property issue is clearly salient here.

On the other hand, the Court ruled that the warrantless monitoring by use of the electronic device in a private dwelling not available to visual surveillance did violate the Fourth Amendment. In the *Knotts* case, the beeper has merely provided some assistance to the visual surveillance of the vehicle as it carried the container over public roads to the defendant's cabin. In the *Karo* case, the beeper had made possible the location of the dwelling, which would not have been established without use of the tracking device. Furthermore, the monitoring over a period of time during which the container was within the private residence had served to provide assurance that it would be there when a search warrant was finally obtained. The Court concluded that, with certain exceptions, the warrantless monitoring of a beeper within a private dwelling amounted to a warrantless search of that dwelling and violated the Fourth Amendment.

Related Constitutional Amendments

Although the Fourth Amendment is most frequently cited in discussions of various monitoring systems, several others bear on the issue. These include the First, the Fifth, the Eighth, the Ninth, and the Fourteenth Amendments. The First Amendment, for example, reads as follows:

> Congress shall make no law respecting an establishment of religion, or prohibiting the free exercise thereof; or abridging the freedom of speech or of the press; or the right of the people peacefully to assemble, and to petition the government for a redress of grievances.

There were no significant Supreme Court interpretations of the First Amendment prior to the Civil War, but Justice Story wrote as early as 1833, that these provisions were intended to secure the rights of "private sentiment" and "private judgement" while the major authority on American public law, Francis Leiber, stressed that these safeguards were crucial to one's "inextinguishable individuality," which might be inhibited if "his communion with his fellows is interrupted or submitted to surveillance" by the "spy, the mouchard, the dilator, the informer, and the sycophant" of "police government" (quoted in Westin, 1967: 331). The First Amendment has often been given priority when there is a conflict among various rights.

Since the *NAACP v. Alabama* (1958) case in the late 1950s, the Supreme Court has applied First Amendment protections more systematically to the defense of the privacy rights of less favored groups. *NAACP v. Alabama* held unconstitutional a requirement that the NAACP reveal its membership and lists of officers as a condition of being admitted as an out-of-state corporation. In this case the Court unanimously declared a right to "associational privacy." The Court reasoned that a forced breach of such associational privacy would very likely subject NAACP members to harassment and thereby interfere with their freedom of speech, their right to assemble, and their right to petition for redress of grievances under the First Amendment.

It is clear that both freedom of speech and freedom of association are considered by the courts to be of fundamental importance. Yet another is absolute. In the case of *Tinker v. Des Moines School District* (1969), for example, certain restrictions on freedom of speech were permitted, given the special nature of the environment. In *Hoffa v. Saxbe* (1974) another district court upheld commutation prohibitions against the indirect or direct management of any labor organization by a particular person with a criminal history.

Among other things, the Fifth Amendment provides that "no person shall be compelled in any criminal case to be a witness against himself, nor be deprived of life, liberty, or property, without due process of law." Fifth Amendment protections against self-incrimination are much more limited than many may believe. Generally, the Supreme Court has interpreted the privilege of any person not to "be compelled in any criminal case to be a witness against himself" to be restricted to forced "testimony." Both federal and state courts have usually held that the Fifth Amendment provides no protection against being compelled to submit to such "self-incriminating" procedures as fingerprinting, photographing, or physical measurements. A person can be compelled to speak or write for purposes of identification. Likewise, a person can be compelled to assume a certain posture or to make a certain gesture. These acts under compulsion are not regarded as the giving of "testimony."

The Eighth Amendment prohibits "cruel and unusual punishments" while the Ninth Amendment states that, "The enumeration in the Constitution of certain rights shall not be construed to deny or disparage others retained by the people." Neither of these is central to the developing legal issues surrounding home confinement at the moment, but each must be considered. The definition of a *cruel and unusual* punishment, as usually interpreted, is that it must be excessive in the sense of involving unnecessary infliction of pain or being grossly out or proportion to the severity of the crime. The stipulation that the enumeration of certain rights must not be regarded as either denying or disparaging others may be interpreted in different ways, ranging from the idea that, "If it's important, why is it not listed?" to the idea that, "Some rights are too obvious to be listed." The nature of the interpretation can become key to the development of the legal concept of privacy.

If Eighth Amendment protections against "cruel and unusual" punishments is to become an issue in connection with home confinement, it will almost certainly have to do with the fact that such court decisions as *Trop v. Dulles* (1958) make reference to evolving standards of decency and progress in suggesting that definitions of what is "cruel" and "unusual" may change over time. Because there is no physical pain involved with home confinement, any Eighth Amendment challenges are likely to have to do with restrictions on travel or issues of personal humiliation and degradation. If the alternative is jail, there appears to be little basis for challenge. But if the alternative might have been a mere curfew, then use of an electronic monitoring bracelet might be challenged, for example, on grounds that it unnecessarily degraded a parent in the eyes of spouse and children also residing in the home, perhaps at the same time contributing to a marital breach and to problems in disciplining the children.

The impact of home confinement on personal privacy and family life may also be raised in terms of the Ninth Amendment, as is indicated in the case of *Griswold v. Connecticut* (1965) described earlier. The executive director of the Planned Parenthood League of Connecticut, Mrs. Estelle Griswold, had been arrested and fined, along with Dr. Charles L. Buxton, the medical director of the League's New Haven center, for providing birth control advice to married couples in violation of Connecticut law. Although the conviction was actually appealed mainly on Fourteenth Amendment grounds, the Supreme Court also cited the First, Third, Fourth, Fifth and Ninth Amendments in striking down the conviction. Both Justice Douglas and Justice Goldberg seemed to adhere to the "some rights are too obvious to be listed" point of view. Justice Douglas maintained that the statement that the enumeration of certain rights as listed in the Bill of Rights "shall not be construed to deny or disparage others retained by the people." Justice Goldberg went even further, pointing out that while some appeared to regard the Ninth Amendment as a recent discovery or to dismiss it as unimportant, it had in fact been a basic part of the original Bill of Rights since 1791. Thus, he insisted, to hold that so basic a right as the right to privacy in marriage may be infringed because it is not referred to specifically in the Bill of Rights is to ignore the Ninth Amendment completely and to give it no effect whatsoever.

The key provisions of the Fourteenth Amendment relevant to home confinement policy are those stipulating "nor shall any state deprive any person of life, liberty, or property without due process of law; nor deny to any person within its jurisdiction the equal protection of the law." In the case of *Edwards v. California* (1941), for example, the Supreme Court relied upon the Fourteenth Amendment as the basis for upholding the right to interstate travel. Generally, the Court has held that the government cannot impose restrictions on the right to travel without showing compelling state interest.

In *Roe v. Wade* (1973) the Supreme Court struck down statutes limiting abortion to therapeutic abortions such as those deemed necessary upon medical advice to save the life of the mother. Several different concurring opinions were written, each tending to rely upon the *liberty* term mentioned in the Fourteenth Amendment and tending to the position that the state interests were not compelling enough to justify such general interference in the personal privacy of the mother as these laws allowed. Otherwise, the various concurring aspects of privacy tended to lay different degrees of stress upon different constitutional aspects of privacy that the Fourteenth Amendment had made applicable to the states.

Both the "due process" and "equal protection of the law" clauses are also relevant here. The "due-process" question becomes the most difficult to resolve in practice, and one of the best ways to deal with the question is to implement new policies through considered legislation rather than through administrative innovation. The "equal protection" clause of the Fourteenth Amendment prohibits the treatment of individuals in such a way as to interfere with the exercise of basic rights or put a given class under a special disadvantage unless there is a legitimate government interest that can withstand strict judicial review. Unless the means of classifying and handling different categories of individuals is inherently invidious or impinges upon a fundamental right, however, it may well be allowed to stand. The Supreme Court has ruled, for example, that classification and differential treatment based upon race, ancestry, or alien status does violate the "equal protection" clause in many instances. The Court tends to view a "suspect class" as one that has been discriminated against historically and appears to be in need of special judicial protection. In addition to race, ancestry, and alien status, the Court has identified gender, indigence, and illegitimacy as categories that *may* be suspect and subject to special scrutiny under the "equal protection" clause.

Diminished Rights of Offenders

The courts have ruled that offenders may not expect the full array of rights accorded ordinary citizens. Home confinement, as now envisioned, involves some degree of due-process hearing by a judicial or administrative officer. Within the confines of correctional institutions, the prisoners retain little in the way of Fourth Amendment protection against "unreasonable search and seizure," such searches and seizures being generally defined as "reasonable" under the circumstances, including the need for institutional security. In the case of *Hudson v. Palmer* (1984), for example, an inmate was denied action under the Fourth Amendment when he alleged that correctional officers intentionally destroyed his personal property during a cell search. In *Morrisey v. Brewer* (1972), a case dealing with the due-process rights of parolees facing revocation, the Supreme Court concluded that the function of parole was a variation on imprisonment accomplished through enforcement of certain conditions. Thus parole is seen as a "conditional liberty," and a lesser degree of constitutional protection is accorded to parolees than to unconvicted citizens with more complete liberty. At the same time, however, the Court recognized that parolees retain many of the basic "core values" of that more complete "liberty," which the incarcerated prisoner has lost by virtue of the different circumstances, and the needs of the correctional institutions.

In the case of *Gagnon v. Scarpelli* (1973), the Court extended to probationers facing revocation the same due-process protections applied to parolees in *Morrisey*. Although it could be argued that parolees were more serious offenders, the Court reasoned that probation was also a functional variation on incarceration that was "constitutionally indistinguishable" from parole as far as due process was concerned. These decisions have, however, continued to give broad discretion to legislatures, sentencing courts, parole boards, and correctional authorities in fixing the terms and conditions of probation and parole. Offenders arrested and released under bond or other conditions before trial have a much stronger argument for full constitutional protections, but in the case of *Bell v. Wolfish* (1979) the Supreme Court has upheld the constitutionality of various confinement conditions imposed on incarcerated pretrial detainees. This decision may have to do with the need for security inside detention facilities, however, as the Court indicated that the supervisory interests of the state over persons charged but not convicted may not include punishment or rehabilitation.

Many jurisdictions have incorporated curfews and other requirements restricting an offender to a certain area as a condition of parole, probation, or pretrial release. In the latter case it may be held that the condition is reasonable as a means of ensuring the appearance of the defendant at trial or protecting the public in the interim. With respect to probation and parole, the situation is clearer. In general, case law appears to show four general elements for a valid set of probation or parole conditions (del Carmen and Vaughn, 1986). These include the stipulations that the conditions involved must be (1) clear, (2) reasonable, (3) constitutional, and (4) protective of society and contributing to the rehabilitation of the offender.

To require that a particular condition be clear means essentially that is must be understandable to the offender. In the case of *Panko v. McCauley* (1979) for example, a condition forbidding a probationer from "frequenting places where alcoholic beverages were sold was struck down on grounds that the term *frequenting* was unclear to the probationer. To be regarded as "reasonable," a condition must be fair and be applied in such a way that the offender can conform. Several cases throw light on the meaning of the reasonableness criterion (del Carmen, 1982). In *Sweeney v. United States* (1965) a condition requiring that a probationer abstain from the use of alcohol for a period of five years was overturned in view of evidence that he was an alcoholic. In *Higdon v. United States* (1980), a condition requiring a former serviceman convicted of accepting kickbacks to forfeit all personal assets and work without pay for a period of three years was struck down as unreasonably harsh as a condition of probation. In *United States v. Jiminez* (1980), a condition ordering a probationer to reimburse the government for the cost of counsel appointed by the court and for the cost of a translator was struck down because it was made a requirement of probation even if the probationer lacked the capacity to pay such costs.

Unconstitutional conditions cannot be set unless there is a valid waiver, but a waiver granted in a situation in which the alternative is jail may not be regarded as voluntary. These constitutional questions may be addressed in turn, beginning with Fourth Amendment issues of search and seizure, which is especially applicable to the monitoring of compliance with the condition of home confinement. In general, it can be said that such monitoring, even with the electronic bracelet, does not at this time constitute a search under the Fourth Amendment, as can be seen from a review of the Fourth Amendment decisions outlined above.

Of course, there are two major differences in the monitoring of home confinement and most of the court decisions described earlier. In the first place, the monitoring of home confinement, whether accomplished through telephone calls, home visits, or electronic means is hardly surreptitious. The monitoring is likely to be more effective in eliciting compliance if the offender is made well aware that he or she is being monitored. Secondly, it is expected that monitoring of home confinement will tend to involve mutual consent. In the case of *Greenholtz v. Nebraska Penal Inmates* (1979) the Supreme Court made it clear that conviction for a crime extinguishes certain constitutional liberties accorded the ordinary citizen. Considering this ruling along with the *Gagnon* and *Morrisey* decisions, lower appellate courts have generally interpreted the law so as to permit even the warrantless search of probationers and parolees and their homes, and this is especially the case where the offender has consented to warrantless searches as a condition of probation or parole.

Court decisions allowing for warrantless searches have tended to proceed on the assumption that in balancing the rights of the offender against the needs of the state, the rights of the offender may be legitimately restricted. First, there is the theory that offenders granted the privilege of a less restrictive alternative than total incarceration should have diminished expectations of privacy. Secondly, there is a stress on the legitimacy of the probation or parole officer's need for information on the activities of the offender (*United States v. Thomas*, 1984; *United States v. Scott*, 1982; *Latta v. Fitzharris*, 1975; *United States ex vel Santos v. New York State Board of Parole*, 1971; *State v. Earnest*, 1980; *State v. Bollinger*, 1971). Yet a minority interpretation exists that would require probation and parole officers to obtain warrants before searching the home on grounds that probationers and parollees have substantially the same Fourth Amendment protections as other citizens have (*United States v. Workman*, 1978; *United States v. Bradley*, 1978).

Court decisions may depend upon not only the question of whether the offender was informed of the possibility of a warrantless search as a condition of probation or parole and whether consent was given, but also upon whether, for example, the search was conducted by a corrections officer within the scope of supervisory duties or by a police officer searching for evidence of criminal activity. In general, however, there appears to be no violation of the Fourth Amendment when there is no interception of actual communication and when the monitoring does not disclose information that could not have been obtained from visual surveillance from outside the home. Theoretically, electronic monitoring would be less intrusive and less dangerous to the Fourth Amendment protections than would be physical search of premises because conversations are not being overheard and evidence of compliance could have been obtained from thorough visual surveillance covering all exits from the home. Practically, however, electronic monitoring would be a more economical means of surveillance than using the police on a 24-hour basis. Therefore, more surveillance and intrusiveness is afforded by electronic monitoring.

Should the courts eventually come to regard electronic monitoring as constituting a "search" under the Fourth Amendment, the question of the legality of warrantless searches could become a very pressing one. In the case of *United States v. Consuelo-Gonzalez* (1975), the Ninth Circuit Court of Appeals ruled that under the Federal Probation Act, federal probationers may be required to submit to warrantless searches by probation officers only. At the same time, however, the decision indicated that the states were free to use different rules in that they were not bound by the Federal Probation Act, and state courts later allowed warrantless searches by both probation officers and police (*State v. Montgomery,* 1977). Some states have been very restrictive as to who may make the warrantless searches and on what grounds (*Utah v. Valasquez,* 1983) while others have allowed much more leeway on both points (*People v. Mason,* 1971).

What if the offender waives Fourth Amendment rights? In the past, the Supreme Court has ruled that an individual may waive such rights beforehand by voluntary action in certain instances. Until recently, courts relied upon express waivers by parolees or probationers, or simply invoked the so-called "act of grace" or "constructive custody" doctrine to deny virtually all Fourth Amendment guarantees to these offenders (del Carmen, 1982). But just how "voluntary" is a waiver obtained under coercive pressure? And how broad a power to engage in warrantless searchers does a waiver grant? In recent years different courts have decided these issues differently, so that the matter is now somewhat confused.

In *United States ex rel. Coleman v. Smith* (1975) a consent to search was thrown out on grounds that the parolee could not be said to have given consent voluntarily in view of the fact that the alternative was eight more years in prison. In the case of *United States v. Bradley* (1978) the Fourth Circuit Court of Appeals overturned a conviction obtained as a result of a search by a parole officer, ruling that the search authority had been used too broadly. Suspecting that a parolee had illegal firearms in his possession, the officer went to his residence under the usual rules of a supervisory visit, but then conducted a search and found a weapon hidden on the premises. The conviction was overturned on grounds that the consent to unannounced, warrantless visits did not extend to consent for thorough searches of the parolee's residence with an aim of discovering incriminating evidence. Later, in the case of *United States v. Workman* (1978), the fourth Circuit Court of Appeals extended this reasoning to apply to probation revocation, thus adding to the weight of authority that holds that Fourth Amendment guarantees do not apply differently in parole and probation cases (del Carmen, 1982).

On the other hand, the courts have not been inclined to invalidate on grounds of coercive pressure consent to warrantless searches obtained from probationers. In *People v. Morgan* (1982), for example, the Nebraska Supreme Court gave the argument some consideration but rejected it, reasoning that if "voluntary" waivers could be overturned because the coercive alternative was a jail sentence, then the coercion rule would strike down all noxious probation conditions whatsoever, making probation unworkable. When a New Mexico probationer advanced a similar argument, it was given no consideration on grounds that probation involved diminished constitutional rights (*State v. Gallagher*, 1984).

As indicated earlier, the courts have been particularly protective of First Amendment rights, treating them as perhaps the most fundamental of all constitutional rights. Much of the opprobrium attached to house arrest stems from the fact that in many societies it is a standard tactic for suppressing political dissent, interfering with freedom of speech, association, and assembly. Thus it may be that given this tradition and the special importance attached to First Amendment rights by courts in the United States, home confinement may come into strict scrutiny in terms of the First Amendment. This is less likely to be the case when home confinement is used along the lines described in the present work than if it is gradually extended as a strategy for dealing with other offenses of a more politically sensitive nature. There is need for real concern over this possibility, and for considerable vigilance as the policy becomes more and more popular.

While probation and parole officers are allowed great leeway in setting conditions for probation or parole, there are important restrictions. The courts tend to uphold the stipulations of conditions that can be shown to contribute in some way to the maintenance of public order or to the rehabilitation of the offender, and these "contributions" are so broadly interpreted as to permit a wide variety of restrictive conditions. Nevertheless, there are limitations. In the case of *Sobell v. Reed* (1971), for example, the New York Board of Parole imposed a condition of parole restricting Sobell's movement to the Southern District of New York, a condition he challenged. The district court ruled that such a condition did represent a violation of Sobell's First Amendment rights to freedom of speech and assembly except in circumstances where the board could show that the restriction was necessary to control specifically described potential misconduct on Sobell's part.

In the *Sobell* case, the parolee had been granted permission to leave the area at a certain time to travel and speak elsewhere, but permission had been denied on other occasions. It was difficult to show that such restrictions on these very fundamental rights of speech and assembly were essential to the protection of the public or a contribution to the parolee's rehabilitation. In the related case of *Hyland v. Procunier* (1970), Hyland had been required, as a condition of parole, to obtain permission from his parole officer before making public speeches, permission that was denied on two occasions when he had asked approval to speak in a public setting on a college campus about prison conditions. These requests had been denied on grounds that such speeches might result in student demonstrations, but the decision in the case held that Hyland's First Amendment rights could not be so abridged.

In cases such as *Porth v. Templar* (1971) this reasoning has also been applied to probation conditions. The condition of probation called into question involved prohibiting a probationer with a history of protesting taxation from speaking or writing on the alleged illegality of the Federal Reserve System and the income tax, and from circulating materials dealing with such subjects. Although the appellate court allowed a condition forbidding the probationer from encouraging violation of the tax laws, it ruled against this more general probation condition as being too sweeping an interference with fundamental constitutional rights.

First Amendment right of association may also be restricted, quite clearly in matters of probation and parole, less clearly in the case of pretrial detainees and others not yet convicted in a court of law. As already indicated, the case of *Hoffa v. Saxbe* (1974) upheld a condition of communication that prohibited the offender from engaging in the direct or indirect management of any labor organization despite the restriction on freedom of association. The Court held that such a restrictive condition was protective of legitimate government interests in view of the offender's history of illegal activity involving labor unions and that its narrow application to association with labor organizations did not strike at free speech or restrict the right of association any more than was necessary for the protection of state interests. In a similar way the courts ruled in *United States v. Tonry* (1979) that a condition prohibiting a former Congressman, who had been convicted for violation of election laws, from engaging in political activity, was not constitutionally improper given his past conduct and the state's interest in protecting the legitimacy of the political process. During the same year, however, an appellate court ruled in *United States v. Furukawa* (1979) against a probation condition that restricted the association of a convicted gambler only to law-abiding citizens (del Carmen, 1982).

Curfew restrictions obviously restrict freedom of association, but the courts may allow them when the restriction appears to contribute to necessary supervision or potential rehabilitation of a probationer or parolee. In the case of *State v. Sprague* (1981), a curfew was upheld when it was determined that it would have the effect of reducing contact with questionable friends during the evening and that such restriction would contribute to the rehabilitation of the probationer. In *State v. Cooper* (1981) a more narrow curfew, prohibiting a probationer from operating a motor vehicle during certain nighttime hours, was upheld. The court agreed that this condition of probation could be defended as a contribution to the protection of the public and the rehabilitation of the probationer in that it would reduce opportunities for criminal contacts.

A citizen's right not to testify against himself or herself is not reduced by conviction. Can home confinement, particularly with the use of the electronic monitoring bracelet, be challenged on grounds that it forces the offender to provide self-incriminating evidence, thereby violating Fifth Amendment protections? As indicated earlier, the courts have generally interpreted the Fifth Amendment as prohibiting forced "testimony" to be used in a court of law. Used in this sense, forced "testimony" seems to imply penetration of the mind by the state. Such physical procedures as fingerprinting or photographing do not involve penetration of the mind and are regarded as acceptable. Electronic bracelets would seem to fall into the same category.

Somewhat related to the electronic monitoring issue are those cases in which a probationer is required as a condition of probation to submit to polygraph tests that might provide incriminating information resulting in new charges. Generally, rulings dealing with Fifth Amendment challenges to such conditions have depended upon (1) whether the government could have reasonably expected to discover incriminating evidence or was engaged in a "fishing expedition," (2) whether use immunity was promised, and (3) whether Fifth Amendment rights had been waived voluntarily—knowingly and intelligently waived (del Carmen, 1982). In the case of *Minnesota v. Murphy* (1984), the Supreme Court ruled that a state may require a probationer to answer incriminating questions if such information contributes to probation supervision and if it is understood that the incriminating evidence may not be used against him or her in new criminal proceedings such as a trial for a new offense.

Here again the legal questions depend to some extent upon the legal status of the offender and the purposes for which the information is to be used. Probation or parole status is different from status as, for example, a pretrial detainee. Monitoring of compliance with a condition of home confinement, whether by telephone contact, visual surveillance, home visits, or electronic bracelets would appear to be well within the Constitution as now interpreted by the courts. It is entirely possible, however, that such evidence as polygraph readings and computer printouts from electronic bracelet signals may one day be treated as "testimony," in which case the extent of legal immunity involved may become a more important issue for the courts.

While it seems highly improbable that home confinement will be effectively challenged on Eighth Amendment grounds of "cruel and unusual punishment," it is interesting to note that the Supreme Court in the case of *Greco v. Georgia* (1976) did make reference to the notion that legal sanctions should be measured against the evolving standards of decency. As far as the law is presently concerned, it is likely that the device will be regarded as fully justifiable in view of the criteria of community protection and contribution to rehabilitation of the offender. The more subtle issue of mortification and degradation through psychological intrusion and the degree to which attachment of a monitoring bracelet to the body is a "punishment" disproportionate to the offense may, however, begin to arise if home confinement is extended to cover offenders who might once have been treated less harshly.

Any examination of constitutional issues associated with home confinement must give particular attention to the Fourteenth Amendment, although there are potential Ninth Amendment questions as well. As noted earlier, the Ninth Amendment stipulates that the enumeration of various constitutional rights shall not be construed "to deny or disparage" other rights retained by the people. The Fourteenth Amendment stipulates that no person shall be deprived of life, "liberty," or property without "due process of law," and guarantees "equal protection of the law." But what are the "liberties" to which the Fourteenth Amendment refers, and to what extent do they include the unnamed "rights" mentioned in the Ninth Amendment?

The right to travel can be restricted as a condition of probation or parole if the restriction can be shown to be reasonable as a contribution to public protection through more effective supervision or as a contribution to the rehabilitation of the offender. It seems highly probable that the Fourteenth Amendment guarantee of "due process" will be seen as central to the implementation of home confinement. As indicated earlier, the courts have ruled that offenders need not be accorded the full array of rights accorded the ordinary citizen. The history of the *Greenholtz* (1979) case offers an interesting illustration of the complexities here (del Carmen, 1982). The Fourteenth Amendment prohibits states from depriving a person of "liberty" without "due process," but what is the meaning of "liberty" for a parolee? Prior to *Greenholtz*, for example, federal appellate courts were sharply divided on this issue. The Third, Fifth, Sixth, Ninth, and Tenth Circuits held that "liberty" was not involved in the context of parole and that due-process rights were therefore inapplicable, but the Second, Fourth, Seventh, and District of Columbia Circuits had ruled otherwise (del Carmen, 1982). In the *Greenholtz* decision the Supreme Court made it clear that conviction for a crime extinguishes certain constitutional rights and that unless a state law created a reasonable expectation rather than a mere hope of parole, a prisoner's constitutional "liberty" is not affected by the release process and due-process rights do not apply. Because Nebraska law read that a prisoner eligible for parole was to be released *unless* certain negating factors happened to exist, the Supreme Court ruled that a reasonable expectation had in fact been created and that due-process guarantees did therefore apply.

Cases since *Greenholtz* make it clear that the nature of due-process guarantees governing release on parole are likely to be narrowly interpreted (del Carmen, 1982). In *Schuemann v. Colorado State Board of Adult Parole* (1980) the Tenth Circuit Court of Appeals ruled that the Colorado law gave broad discretion as to whether the Board should release on parole and created no reasonable expectation that would invoke due-process rights. But even where due-process rights are applied, they may not extend as far as those accorded ordinary citizens in a court of law, stopping short, for example, of granting a prisoner access to his file. The difference between the *Schuemann* case and the *Morrisey* decision on the "liberty" of parolees or the *Gagnon* decision on the "liberty of probationers is that the latter two decisions dealt with offenders who were already in a situation of "conditional liberty." The "conditional liberty" of home confinement may fall somewhere between the lack of liberty experienced by an institutionally incarcerated prisoner and the more complete liberty experienced by an ordinary probationer.

The "equal protection" clause of the Fourteenth Amendment will also come into play in the administration of home confinement policy. Problems could arise here in the event that there is differential handling of offenders by race, ancestry, alien status, gender, illegitimacy, indigence, or some other "suspect class." The courts are inclined to scrutinize with greater care situations in which there has been differential handling of different classes of offenders when history shows a pattern of past discrimination. The Supreme Court has struck down discriminatory classifications justified by "administrative convenience" or "public interest" as insufficiently compelling (*Graham v. Richardson*, 1971). In the case of *Bearden v. Georgia* (1983), the Supreme Court held that probation cannot be revoked because of inability to pay a fine and make restitution as a condition of the probation if the failure is a result of indigence rather than refusal to pay, and if probation is adequate to ensure governmental interests. In situations where an offender is denied home confinement because he or she cannot afford a telephone or cannot meet the cost of an electronic bracelet, the "equal protection" clause of the Fourteenth Amendment will sooner or later arise.

There is, however, one final consideration that may render moot many of the issues discussed. This is the fact that home confinement, with or without electronic monitoring, generally involves the *consent* of the offender. Court decisions cited above have upheld the "installation" of electronic devices when done with the consent of the person involved. While it is true that consent to conditions governing home confinement may be somewhat less than "voluntary" when the alternative is institutional detention or incarceration, the courts have usually approved agreements in which the state conditions a less severe punishment upon the relinquishment of certain basic rights. In this view, it is only "reasonable" that the probationer forego such basic constitutional rights as can be shown to serve the protection of the public and the rehabilitation of the offender. And, as indicated earlier, the courts take a very broad view here, in that almost any condition can be shown to protect the public or make a possible contribution to the rehabilitation of the offender.

Without such a liberal interpretation of "consent," the courts would probably not be able to function at all. Thus certain elements of the *crime control model* of criminal justice come to be regarded as necessities. Consider the Sixth Amendment, which reads:

> In all criminal prosecutions, the accused shall enjoy the right to a speedy and public trial, by an impartial jury of the state and district wherein the crime shall have been committed, which district shall have been previously ascertained by law, and be informed of the nature and cause of the accusation; to be confronted with the witnesses against him; to have compulsory process for obtaining witnesses in his favor, and to have the assistance of counsel for his defense.

But, of course, things do not work this way in practice. Only 1 criminal conviction in 10 has been obtained by way of a jury trial involving confrontation with witnesses and the other constitutionally guaranteed rights of the alleged offender. This is because of the very widespread use of plea bargaining. In *Brady v. United States* (1971), the Supreme Court ruled that the government may compel a defendant to surrender Sixth Amendment rights to a jury trial and Fifth Amendment rights against self-incrimination in return for accepting a guilty plea to a lesser offense. If the person who receives such a "bargain" later challenges the terms of the agreement, and if all other parts of the waiver or consent have been met, the individual is regarded as having waived the rights in question. The same interpretation is made in cases where a probationer or parolee has received a suspension of sentence or reduction in length of commitment in return for surrendering constitutional rights (*United States v. Mitsubishi International Corporation*, 1982; *Carchedi v. Rhodes*, 1982).

Some Additional Legal Issues

To this point, the examination of legal issues facing home confinement has focused upon the rights of the offender. But what happens to others living in the home when it is transformed into the offender's jail? Clearly, they retain all of the rights and privileges of any citizen. Yet there are some potential legal problems here, and they must be given at least cursory consideration.

One problem has to do with the possibility that others in the home may be victimized by the offender. It would be obviously questionable policy to place in home confinement, for example, a violent husband just convicted of spouse abuse. Careful screening of offenders is the best approach to ensuring that they do not abscond, victimize others in the home, or fail in any other way to comply with the conditions of home confinement. Still, even the most careful screening cannot be expected to be completely error free.

The guiding principle in screening so as to avoid the victimization of others in the home is likely to be the same as that generally applied to decisions made by probation and parole officers, decisions that are expected to take account of risks to the public. This principle has been called that of the "reasonably foreseeable risk" (del Carmen, 1982: 45). Four different cases throw considerable light on the legal issues associated with the concept of the "reasonably foreseeable" type of risk that a probation or parole officer may be expected to avoid and for the results of which they may be held legally accountable. These are the *Johnson, Goergen, Rieser,* and *Meyers* cases (del Carmen, 1982: 42-45).

In *Johnson v. State* (1968) a parolee had been placed with a foster parent who was later assaulted by the parolee. The foster parent brought suit, charging that she had not been properly warned of the parolee's past violence and potential for homicidal tendencies. The California Supreme Court ruled that the state was liable for the injuries because the parole officer had been aware of the parolee's history of violence and his homicidal tendencies, should therefore have known that the Johnson family might be endangered, and yet had failed to inform the foster parent of the foreseeable risk entailed in taking the parolee into the home. A similar decision was handed down in the case of *Goergen v. State* (1959) where the New York Division of Parole was held liable for failing to inform the assaulted plaintiff of the violent background of a parolee when recommending him for employment.

The case of *Reiser v. District of Columbia* (1977) grew out of a situation in which a parolee had been assisted by the District of Columbia Department of Corrections in obtaining employment at an apartment complex. At the time of parole he was a suspect in two rape-murder cases. During his employment at the apartment complex itself, he became a suspect in a third murder case. The parole officer had given no warning to the parolee's employer of any possible danger, but the employer had later been informed by the police as to the parolee's criminal record and suspected involvement in the three homicides. Not long after this notification by the police, the parolee entered the room of a young woman living in the apartment complex, where he raped and killed her. The mother of the victim brought suit and was awarded damages. The decision was appealed, but the appellate court upheld the award, ruling that the parole officer had a duty to inform the employer of the parolee's record of sex-related violence, particularly in view of the fact that the employment made him a virtual member of the extended "household" where many women resided, and gave him access to information about their personal habits and potential access to keys to their residences.

The case of *Meyers v. Los Angeles County Probation Department* (1978) was somewhat different. Here the court ruled that the probation department was *not* liable in a situation where the probation officer had not informed an employer of the probationer's conviction for embezzlement and the probationer proceeded to embezzle from this new employer as well. One difference between the *Meyers* case and those of *Johnson, Goergen,* and *Reiser* is the fact that the former did not entail the reasonably foreseeable risk of exposing uninformed persons to potential *violence* on the part of dangerous offenders. The more significant difference, however, is the fact that in *Meyers* the probation department had not placed the offender with the particular employer and had in no other way established a "special relationship" between the department and the employer (del Carmen, 1982: 45).

The concept of a "reasonably foreseen risk" appears to involve at least three separate but related aspects: (1) The notion that some "special relationship" has been established that increases the obligation of the officer to "foresee" risks; (2) the notion that the nature of the relationship is such that the officer can "reasonably foresee" that the offender may commit an offense similar to that committed in the past; and (3) that this risk involves the possibility of danger to a specific potential victim or victims rather than to the public at large. Thus in *Johnson,* a "special relationship" and special obligation to inform had been established as a result of the parole officials' convincing the potential victim to take on the role of foster parent. Something similar had happened in *Goergen,* where the officials had urged the plaintiff to hire the parolee, and in *Reiser,* where the parole officials not only helped the parolee secure the job with the specific employer, but allowed him to remain on that job as evidence of sex-related violence continued to develop. In *Meyers,* on the other hand, state officials had not helped the probationer find and secure the particular job in which another embezzlement was eventually undertaken.

As to that aspect of the concept of a "reasonably foreseeable risk," which involves the notion that the officer can "reasonably foresee" the risk that the offender may commit an offense similar to that committed in the past, it is clear that one cannot be expected to "reasonably foresee" a convicted rapist being likely to commit an embezzlement in a new job or an embezzler placed with a specific employer in a "special relationship" being likely to commit a rape there. One can be expected only to take into account past history. More than that, this notion also revolves around the assumption that the circumstances in which the offender is placed by circumstances increasing the risk that past offenses will be repeated or that offenses similar to them may be forthcoming. Placement of a parolee with a history of sex-related violent crimes on a job in an apartment complex housing many women to whose personal lives and residences he has potential access is the clearest example.

Unless the third aspect of the concept of a "reasonably foreseeable risk" is applied, it would become impossible to release many offenders to probation or parole. Here too, the matter of a "special relationship" becomes salient. Any time a potentially dangerous offender is placed on probation or parole, the general public is endangered. While there have been cases in which the faulty supervision of a probationer or parolee has been held to make an officer or agency liable for dangers posed to the general public (del Carmen, 1982), the general rule is that the "reasonably foreseeable risk" must be to a specific victim or victims. Thus the release of the parolee in the *Johnson* case posed some danger to the community at large, but the liability became an issue because the placing of that offender in the home of specific individuals in a "special relationship" with both the parole officials and the parolee himself made it considerably more probable that one of the members of this specific family was being placed at risk. In a similar way, the employer in *Goergen* was a specific individual being placed at risk and the women residing in the apartment complex in *Reiser* were a specific group of potential victims placed at risk because of his employment there.

These cases bear upon home confinement because such a policy would seem to bring into play all of the aspects of the concept of a "reasonably foreseen risk" outlined above. Confining the offender to the home would appear to establish a "special relationship" among the agency doing the confining, the offender, and others residing in the home, and it would also appear to place at risk a specific potential victim or victims rather than the community at large. The key therefore seems to lie in the screening of offenders placed in home confinement in such a way as to minimize the risk that someone in the home would be victimized by an offense identical with, similar to, or in some way related to an offense previously committed by the person confined. It is obvious that an offender convicted of spouse abuse may pose a problem when confined in a tiny apartment with his wife and forbidden to leave the premises for even a few minutes, but other risks may not turn out to be so clear-cut.

A second set of problems has to do with the possibility that others in the home may in certain circumstances be placed under pressure to cooperate with the offender in more or less serious violations of the conditions of the home confinement. This might arise, for example, in a situation where a drug abuser had developed a pattern of driving to a certain part of town to make contact with a dealer, make a buy, and then to go a hotel room where the drug use occurs. It is plausible that, as a condition of probation, this person, if convicted, would be required to avoid any further drug use under penalty of revocation. If confined to the home, it is also plausible that the offender might, through threats, actual violence, offers of money, or some other inducement, persuade another person in the home to drive to the usual location, make the drug purchase, and bring it to him or her. Not only has that person now become an accomplice in violation of the conditions of probation, but he or she is now involved in serious, criminal activity and might easily be arrested for possession if the probationer is on supervisory surveillance. In extreme cases where it is "reasonable" to expect that the probationer may bring some pressure on others in the home to assist in the procurement of drugs, and where surveillance over the home might "reasonably" be expected to add to the likelihood that offenses committed by others living there would be detected, facilitation might even be changed. The answer here also lies in careful screening of offenders placed in home confinement, which keeps very much in mind the effect of the situation on others residing in the home.

GENERAL SOCIAL ISSUES

Beyond the legal issues, both broad and narrow, surrounding the question of home confinement, there are some very profound social issues. Indeed, there is something that troubles many when the matter of house arrest arises. And these nagging doubts become sharper and sharper when new technologies such as electronic monitoring enter the scene. It would be irresponsible of those investigating the increasing popularity of home confinement not to give some critical reflection to deeper social issues, for these issues might well become more and more pressing as home confinement spreads and becomes a strategy of choice in dealing with a wide variety of offenders.

There are several ways in which the deeper social issues might be approached, and it is the intention of the authors to provide at some later opportunity an extended treatment of the sort that is beyond the scope of the present work. Here we will confine ourselves to an approach that deals with some social issues in terms of the concept of *privacy*. This concept has a (very muddled) legal meaning and a (not very precise) social psychological meaning. Some students of the privacy problem have recognized the connection between the two provinces of meaning and some have not. One would expect them to disagree as to the possible effects of widespread home confinement, especially involving electronic monitoring.

A purely legal focus would probably conclude that home confinement presents no social or philosophical problems whatsoever as long as the monitoring is not surreptitious, the offender being aware of it and having given voluntary consent to it. But there are larger issues. What does it imply when homes are being converted into jails? What will be the effect of a policy that might lead to a significant portion of society living under the constant realization that their movement is being monitored by a computer somewhere? Is this just the beginning of what will become further state intrusion into the home? Is it part of an even larger trend toward greater state control over the private lives of its citizens? Such questions as these should be addressed as early as possible in the development of a new criminal and juvenile justice alternative. It may not be possible to answer them, but the questions are "sensitizing." They force us to be sensitive to the larger implications of our efforts, to the "big picture." And they may lead to additional questions that should be asked.

With respect to the question of privacy itself, it is instructive to note that legal scholars disagree as to whether or not a citizen of the United States has a *distinct* right to privacy. The so-called "reductionists" maintain that there is no such right that can be set forth as distinct from some more fundamental right such as might adhere to property. Others insist that there is such a right in itself, perhaps not specifically cited in the Constitution precisely because it is so fundamental as to be taken for granted. Still, even among those who insist that the right to privacy is basic, there is considerable disagreement as to why this is the case. The result is that the concept of privacy is a point of much contention, and privacy law can be described as akin to "a haystack in a hurricane" (*Ettore* v. Philco Television Broadcasting Co., 1956).

Although, as Westin (1967) has pointed out, the notion of personal privacy was of some importance to the framers of the Constitution, there is no specific mention of it there. It has become fashionable to trace the legal concept of privacy in constitutional law to a classic article by Warren and Brandeis (1890), perhaps because Brandeis later became one of the most famous and respected of Supreme Court justices. Definitions of privacy vary somewhat, however, depending upon where the stress is laid. Westin (1967: 254) defines privacy in terms of information, holding that, "Privacy is the claim of individuals, groups, or institutions to determine for themselves when, how, and to what extent information about themselves is communicated to others." The political import of privacy comes through very clearly in Altman's (1974: 6) definition of privacy as "the negation of potential power relationships between a person or group and others."

There have been empirical studies of privacy, and they are very suggestive in that they tend to take into account the definition or meaning of privacy to the individual, something that the law usually ignores (Levin and Askin, 1977). Wolfe and Laufer (1974) found that privacy carries four related meanings, including (1) controlling access to information about oneself, (2) being alone, (3) "no one bothering me," and (4) controlling access to spaces. All of these meanings seem relevant to home confinement, particularly with the omnipresent electronic monitoring devices, and the importance of the personal experience of privacy in such settings has been stressed by many students of human behavior. During the 1960s the Warren Court, as part of the more general movement to protect the rights of individuals, departed somewhat from the usual legal practice of ignoring the meaning of privacy to those involved. The *Katz* decision is an example, not only because it held that "the Fourth Amendment protects people, not places," but also because it contained a legal appreciation for the subjective experience of the individual, the "actual expectation of privacy," in a given situation.

The experience of privacy is of great social psychological significance. That is why the concept of privacy is so closely associated with the notion of the autonomous individual. The social psychological development of the "self" is a product of history. The very concept of a private, autonomous, inner "self" appears to have developed through the physical and emotional seclusion coming with the "privacy" attained when home, in general, came to be constructed and used so as to place certain areas outside the public domain (Shorter, 1977). Prior to this development, it was common for outsiders to roam through the home at will. There was little in the way of privacy in the modern sense, and anyone seeking such might have been thought odd.

It is no accident that the slogan, "A man's home is his castle," has taken on such significance in Anglo-American thought. As time passed, the home took on a sacred character. It became a personal sanctuary and a bastion of political freedom. It became a symbol of the personal dignity of the individual, no matter his or her station in life. Thus the famous and often cited quotation from William Pitt:

> The poorest man may in his cottage bid defiance to the crown. It may be frail—its roof may leak—the wind may enter—but the King of England cannot enter—all his force dares not cross the threshold of the ruined tenement [Quoted in Glasser, 1974: 100].

If the sense of human dignity and personal autonomy and even the political and legal concept of the "rights of the individual" are dependent to some extent upon a deeper sense of privacy associated with defending the boundaries of the home, to what extent may these be diminished by a policy that makes the home the offender's jail? This is an important question. It is worth pointing out that legal concepts of the rights of individual privacy revolve around some assumption of the responsibility of institutions, however powerful, to avoid potential intrusion (Levin and Askin, 1977). Under many circumstances it may require a strong sense of personal dignity and self-respect to make such challenges, so that any erosion of this sense of autonomy may operate to encourage further intrusion, which may then encourage a vicious cycle in which the concepts of personal dignity and self-respect become dim memories. Some have argued that such is the drift of history as we move toward the "carceral society," which is itself a vast prison (Foucault, 1977).

Because of the importance of the home to the sense of human dignity and autonomous selfhood, we have been concerned from the beginning of our efforts to explore the potential of home confinement as an alternative with the social psychological implications (Ball and Lilly, 1983a, 1983b). Even the use of volunteers to monitor compliance by telephone presents problems, for the telephone itself alters the social psychology of human relationships and makes possible an invasion of privacy (Ball, 1968). The telephone has been described as an "irresistible intruder in time and place" (McLuhan, 1965: 271). Unless the call is obscene, threatening, or especially annoying, however, we have become such "slaves" to the device that almost no one can find strength to resist its ring (Ball, 1968).

The electronic monitoring devices seem to hold a special fascination for some while evoking an uneasy distaste in others, although neither group seems able to articulate its response very clearly. Those who respond negatively often mention the "Orwellian" aspect, and we ourselves have referred to the "Orwellian overtones" associated with electronic monitoring within a "sacred ground off-limits to the state except under extreme conditions" (Ball and Lilly, 1983a: 17). The electronic bracelet is intrusive in a different way than is the telephone, not only because it is strapped to the *body* itself. This is a significant difference because the body is even more crucial to selfhood than is the home.

In his analysis of the legal concept of privacy as presented in an influential article by Prosser (1960), Bloustein (1964) has taken an approach more typically taken by social scientists or philosophers than by law professors or the courts. Asking what Warren and Brandeis (1890) meant in their classic call for the legal recognition of privacy rights, Bloustein points out that they refer to the right to privacy as a "spiritual" rather than a "material" right and hold it to be especially important in protection of "inviolate personality." As he says, the right to privacy protects not simply some property right such as reputation, but individuality itself. Thus "A man whose home may be entered at the will of another, whose conversation may be overheard at the will of another, whose marital and familial intimacies may be overseen at the will of another, is less of a man, has less human dignity, on that account" (Bloustein, 1964: 971). Furthermore, the question of social power is of central significance to privacy, because "He who may intrude upon another at will is the master of the other and, in fact, intrusion is a primary weapon of the tyrant" (Bloustein, 1964: 971).

As has been noted elsewhere in this volume, electronic monitoring has a history going back to the 1960s. In response to issues arising at that time, Fried (1968) has undertaken an analysis of privacy that attempts to go beyond the criticisms that were leveled at the early movement toward electronic monitoring. It is true, as he notes, that cautions about information falling into the wrong hands must be considered, that opportunities for harassment are presented, that the monitoring may draw in those not really in need of such intense supervision, that there are dangers to political expression and association, and so forth. "And yet one often wants to say the invasion of privacy is wrong, intolerable, although each discrete objection can be met" (Fried, 1968: 477). This is because according a fundamental right to privacy in itself is according respect to the individual human being apart from any economic property rights or political rights to free speech and association, respect that is essential as a basis for the building of such social psychological experiences as friendship and love. Such experiences as friendship and love are neither economic nor political experiences. They are moral experiences. According to Fried, it is not possible to experience genuine friendship or love for one who is not first respected *as a person*, as a human subject, rather than as the mere bearer of certain abstract economic and political rights granted, for example, by a document such as the Constitution.

As noted earlier, the basis of legal concepts of the rights of privacy revolve around the idea of the individual's right to challenge intrusions rather than around some assumption of the responsibility of institutions, such as the state, to avoid potential intrusions. But privacy is not merely a defensive right. It is a mistake to consider privacy as a right granted to the individual by the political state. Privacy is rather the basis of individuality. "It rather forms the necessary context for the intimate relations of love and friendship that gives our lives much of whatever affirmative value they have" (Fried, 1968: 498). Although not as clearly articulated, it is very likely that this affirmative approach to privacy is the fundamental recognition lying behind assertions that the right of privacy is "older than the Bill of Rights."

Fried makes still another point worth considering. Despite the criticism that can be leveled at home confinement, with or without electronic monitoring, there is always the counterargument that it is better than institutional detention, jail, or prison, all of which are much more intrusive and much less protective of personal privacy. That is essentially true. On the other hand, it is important to recognize that detention centers, jails, and prisons are overtly unprivate, presenting contexts obviously different from those on the "outside." Under conditions of home confinement, particularly with electronic monitoring, there is the *appearance* of freedom and autonomy without the substance. "If the prisoner has a reasonably developed capacity for love, trust, and friendship, and has in fact experienced ties of this sort, he is likely to be strongly aware (at least for a time) that prison life is a drastically different context from the one in which he enjoyed those relations, and this awareness will militate against his confusing the kinds of relations that can obtain in a 'total institution' like a prison with those of freer setting on the outside" (Fried, 1968: 499). Home confinement may tend to blur this otherwise clear distinction.

Reiman (1976: 38) has gone even further in advancing the argument that privacy is fundamental to the development of "personhood." According to Reiman (1976: 38), *"Privacy is a social ritual by means of which an individual's moral title to this existence is conferred."* (italics in the original). Through the social practice of privacy, society recognizes and communicates to the individual "that this existence is his own," the recognition of which is "a precondition of personhood" (Reiman, 1976: 38). This argument is quite explicit in basing itself to a considerable extent upon the social scientific theory of symbolic interactionism a perspective that makes the human subject interactionism, a perspective that makes the human subject central. "And if one takes—as I am inclined to—the symbolic interactionist perspective that teaches that 'selves' are created in social interaction rather than flowering innately from inborn seeds, to this claim is added an even stronger one: privacy is necessary to the creation of *selves* out of human beings, since a self is at least in part a human being who regards his existence—his thoughts, his body, his actions—as his *own.*" (Reiman, 1976: 38. Emphasis in the original).

Speaking of the relationship of the person to the body, Reiman (1976: 38) points out that "A social order in which bodies were held to others, to or to the collectivity, and in which individuals grew up believing that their bodies were not theirs from a moral point of view, is conceivable." There are said to be two essential conditions of moral ownership of one's body. The first is the right to do with the body what one wishes. The second is the right to control when and by whom one's body is experienced. Both involve the sense of one's body belonging to oneself rather than to another, and in a much deeper sense than mere property right. "The right to privacy, then, protects the individual's interest in becoming, being, and remaining a person" (Reiman, 1976: 44).

Gavison (1980) gets even closer to the heart of the matter in her careful analysis of the functions of privacy. As she points out, privacy is more than a question of personal control over revelations about oneself or the negation of power-relationships between oneself and others. The value placed on privacy may have nothing to do with whether the individual has chosen it. A person might choose to engage in sexual intercourse in a public place, but most people would probably criticize this behavior. One reason is that such activity is considered degrading to the particular person and to human beings in general. It is thought to be a violation of human dignity and a demonstration of a lack of respect for oneself, *especially* if freely chosen. This may explain, in part, the uneasiness experienced when one observes the eagerness of an offender in surrendering to the state not only access to the home but even access to the body in return for leniency.

If the legal issues surrounding house arrest are complex, the social issues are even more complicated. The home detention programs for youths described in Chapters 2 and 3 do not seem particularly problematic, but the image of adult controlees whose presence is constantly monitored by a central computer linked to a body bracelet can be disquieting. The social psychological implications deserve considerable attention. Indeed, any tendency to extend the electronic monitoring as a means of controlling behavior that would formerly have been ignored may be expected of bringing up serious legal as well as social questions associated with the concept of privacy.

6

Conclusion

As a correctional policy, house arrest offers a real alternative. Yet it would be a mistake to consider this option as free from risks. As we have indicated elsewhere in this volume, it is our intention to devote an additional volume to a consideration of the potential dangers of any trend toward extremely widespread use of home confinement. Because such a treatment demands a somewhat exhaustive sociohistorical and social psychological analysis, it is far beyond the scope of what can be attempted here. It is possible, however, to present some preliminary consideration, and we will turn in that direction after having laid out what appears to be the principal advantages of house arrest as an alternative correctional policy.

GENERAL ADVANTAGES
OF HOME CONFINEMENT

As a new option, home confinement offers an inherently flexible set of possibilities that provide a good fit to many existing programs in such a way as to make them even more effective. This is because house arrest can be structured for different times of day, different periods during the week, and from periods ranging from perhaps less than a month to a total of two years. The various programs described in Chapters 2, 3, and 4 demonstrate that such structuring works in practice as well as in theory, and our examination of legal issues in Chapter 5 suggests that various arrangements will be legally acceptable as long as they can be justified as protecting the community and contributing to the rehabilitation of the offender in some reasonable way.

Thus it is possible to "ground" youths in a home detention program, such as that in Cuyahoga County, Ohio, during specific

periods of the day and even on weekends so as to ensure that they will
be available to the court and reduce the likelihood of further offenses.
Although there has been some dispute as to whether such a sentence is
"expecting too much," the Florida programs have shown that judges
are willing to impose a sentence of home confinement for a period of
as long as two years. It is important for moral, practical, and legal
viewpoints, however, that the periods and related conditions set be
"reasonable," morally, practically, and legally, rather than being
developed in some arbitrary or biased fashion. Terms set in an
arbitrary or biased way are morally indefensible. Furthermore, they
are not likely to achieve the practical results of community protection
and offender rehabilitation if they appear to be unreasonable.
Finally, it is clear that they are subject to legal challenge.

The flexibility of home confinement as a correctional policy
means that it can be used as one component of a tailored package
suitable to a particular offender. Thus, for example, home detention
as described in Chapters 2 and 3 might be sufficient in itself. If, on the
other hand, a particular youth had been adjudicated delinquent,
home confinement might be combined with restitution or community
service, especially in certain cases such as those involving serious
vandalism. The home confinement would serve to protect the
community and to assuage community outrage and demand for
"punishment." The restitution and community service would serve
to repair the damage done and perhaps to contribute to the
rehabilitation of the offender, at least to a greater extent than would
institutional incarceration.

One of the clearest illustrations of the way in which home
confinement can be used us a "tailored package," may be seen in its
use as a policy for dealing with drunken driving (Ball and Lilly,
1983b, 1986a). What the community seems to want most here is
protection from drunken drivers. Because other policies, ranging
from revocation of a driver's license to special plates and ignition
control devices, have failed, the public has tended to demand
mandatory jailing. This in turn has resulted in even more severe
overcrowding of jails, to the extent that motels, vacant buildings, and
even high school gymnasiums have been converted into "jails"
housing DWI offenders doing weekend "jail" terms. There are
simply not enough facilities to meet this demand.

Furthermore, jail incarceration may be the last thing one ought to
do with many drunken drivers. Some are youthful first offenders

whose jail incarceration subjects them to gang rape and other violence. Some are middle-class housewives suffering from a clinical depression of which the drinking is a symptom; to jail them for a weekend is hardly likely to aid in recovery (Ball and Lilly, 1986a). Others are chronic alcoholics whose drinking is otherwise considered an illness for which they cannot be jailed, but who are jailed if apprehended while driving. Home confinement allows for the restriction of such offenders in such a way as to protect the community, at the same time allowing them to participate in alcohol education and treatment programs and hold a job. Experience to date with the programs described in Chapter 4 suggests that home confinement may be very effective in dealing with the DWI problem.

Another major advantage of home confinement as a correctional policy lies in the fact that it can be employed at virtually any stage in the process of dealing with offenders. Chapters 2 and 3 make it very clear that home detention offers solid possibilities as a policy for handling offenders even prior to adjudication. Chapter 4 provides an indication of the way in which home incarceration can be used as an alternative sentence, a condition of probation, or a condition for participation in a work release program on the part of institutionally incarcerated offenders. The legal issues involved are somewhat different in each case, but as long as this is kept in mind, home confinement or house arrest seems to offer different sorts of possibilities at every stage in the criminal or juvenile justice processes.

One of the advantages of home confinement that has not been realized up to now, is the way in which it might be developed so the practice could be easily initiated by the offender as well as by the authorities. It is obvious from the foregoing chapters that home confinement can be developed allowing for easy initiation by the court in situations, for example, where a particular judge considers it the best alternative. From the beginning of our own efforts in this area, however, we have urged legislation that would make it relatively simple for the impetus for home confinement to be initiated by *petition from the offender*. There are many offenders who might find it in their best interests to petition the court for home confinement, and it is possible to draft legislation that would force the court to consider this alternative in certain cases. Such offenders include, for example, the mentally retarded, who would be at a severe disadvantage in jail, but who could be supervised in the home; the terminally ill; and perhaps others whose offenses might involve extenuating circumstances that either were inadmissible at trial or did not provide a satisfactory legal defense to the charges. If home confinement is to be offered to the authorities as an option, perhaps it should be offered to the citizen as well, assuming it can be justified.

SPECIFIC ADVANTAGES
OF HOME CONFINEMENT

While home confinement offers some general advantages as an alternative correctional policy in that it can be combined with other programs, applied at virtually any stage in the criminal or juvenile justice process, and eventually initiated by either the authorities or the offender, these advantages will not ensure its adoption. More important is the fact that home confinement appears to possess all the attributes deemed crucial by the National Advisory Commission on Criminal Justice Standards and Goals for the Criminal Justice System (1973) in determining the actual expectation for adoption of a new criminal or juvenile alternative. These include the *communicability* of the policy, its *complex level*, its *potential impact,* the fact that it is characterized by *reasonable cost,* its inherent *reversibility* and *divisibility*, its *compatibility* with existing programs, and its *perceived relevance to organizational goals.*

In terms of *communicability*, home confinement is a concept that is easy to understand. It is possible to communicate the idea in very simple language without the proliferation of jargon that so often confuses criminal and juvenile justice policy. It has its precedents in the idea of the "curfew" and even the traditional vernacular by which we refer to the "grounding" of an adolescent as punishment for certain infractions. Beyond the general idea, the specifics of various conditions set for home confinement are also relatively easy to communicate. As home confinement continues to develop, it will become more important that specific terms such as *home detention* and *home incarceration* be employed with some accuracy. As we have indicated, this is one problem with the term *ouse arrest.* It may be satisfactory as a means of communicating the concept to the general public, but even this is somewhat questionable. More careful use of the few key terms surrounding home confinement will assist greatly in allowing those involved in the development and implementation of the policy to communicate clearly with one another as to the exact nature of what is being proposed.

As for the *complexity level* of home confinement as a new alternative, the efforts reviewed in earlier chapters seem to indicate that the policy is of minimum complexity. If it is developed and implemented by legislation, the legal research involved is not unduly complicated. As Chapter 5 points out, there are certainly some legal issues to be faced, but they are no more complex than in most areas of criminal and juvenile law. We have attempted to illustrate the lack of administrative complexity by including in the appendices specific examples of relevant legislation as well as sample forms from different programs. An examination of these materials will show that home confinement is not an especially complex alternative to develop and implement. Our hope is that the materials contained in the appendices will make this clear while contributing further to an understanding of the way in which the policy is actually administered on a day-to-day basis.

The *potential impact* of home confinement is fairly clear and somewhat easier to measure than the impact of many other correctional alternatives. This is the case, of course, if the consideration of potential impact is defined in the usual terms. It is not so clear if greater attention is given to the sociohistorical and social psychological aspects of home confinement. But these issues are far beyond the scope of this volume. As we have indicated elsewhere, there is an obligation to consider these "deeper" implications and "potential impact," and we intend to do that in another place. This will tend to involve considerable speculation, which is something we have tried to avoid here, preferring to lay out the current developments as clearly as possible, while only touching upon certain cautionary notes. We feel that it will be best to defer deeper probing until enough time has passed for a clearer picture to emerge as to the types of offenders to whom home confinement will be extended and the conditions, including electronic monitoring, under which it will be applied.

If potential impact is defined in the usual terms, however, it seems to be fairly clear and relatively easy to measure in the case of home confinement. The data presented in Chapters 2, 3, and 4 provide a picture of the potential impact of both home detention for youths and home incarceration for adults. While several different definitions of *success* may be employed, it is not especially difficult to achieve a reasonable measure of the impact of the policy once success is defined.

Records will indicate numbers of offenders placed in home confinement, periods of such confinement, instances of either technical violation of the conditions of home confinement or commission of new offenses, and will provide other data necessary to evaluate impact.

The question of potential impact is, of course, different from that of actual impact. For example, the *potential* impact of home confinement on jail depopulation may turn out to be quite different from the actual impact, depending upon the extent to which judges use the alternative and the types of offenders to whom the alternative is applied. In Kenton County, Kentucky, for example, the *potential* impact of home incarceration on jail depopulation has not been realized, partly because the judges may not be using it as an alternative to jail, but as another option short of jailing, and partly because so little use has been made of it at all. As indicated in Chapter 4, however, caution is perhaps to be expected in the early stages of experimentation with a different policy. It may be that the next few years will show that the potential impact has become a reality.

The nature of the impact of home confinement, whether home detention of juveniles or home incarceration (for example, in-house arrest) of adults is clearer in the data presented in Chapter 3, relative to the practice in Cuyohoga County, Ohio, and in Chapter 4, at the point where Florida programs are considered. One of the serious questions relating to the potential impact of home confinement has revolved around possible public reaction to the policy. It seemed clear from the earliest experiments that adverse reaction on the part of the media and the general public would result in reluctance to implement the policy at all, or token implementation, either of which would mean that any impact would have been minimal. To this point, however, both media reaction and general public reaction has been very favorable, suggesting that home confinement may have more and more effect as time passes.

The potential impact of home confinement can be seem especially clearly upon an examination of its use in dealing with offenders such as drunken drivers (Ball and Lilly, 1983b, 1986a). The data presented in Chapter 4 provide some indication of how such a policy may operate. One of the problems in dealing with the drunken driver lies in the fact that the courts are reluctant to convict offenders when jailing is involved, leading to a tendency to plea-bargain the charges down to reckless driving (Ball and Lilly, 1986a). Many factors lead the court to avoid the imposition of a sentence deemed too harsh, including empathy for the driver, concern over a possible job loss, and fear as to what may await the offender in the jail. The result of the plea bargaining is that habitual drunken drivers are always first offenders because prior convictions will refer to a history of reckless driving but show no pattern of drunken driving at all. Thus the idea of a mandatory jail term sounds good in theory, but turns out in practice in sheltering the drunken driver. The availability of home incarceration as an alternative sentence allows the court to establish the drunken driving, get it on the record, and provide protection to the community, while avoiding the problems associated with jailing.

Even if the courts were eager to prosecute and convict drunken drivers, there is the problem of a heavy backlog of cases along with a shortage of judges. Because the drunken driver is often a middle-class person with a job and family, he or she may be expected to hire an attorney and demand a trial when faced with a potentially severe sentence such as jail (Galvin et al., 1974). The availability of home incarceration allows for an alternative that may appeal to the offender. Indeed, the data reported in Chapter 4 suggest that programs, such as those of Pride, Inc. in Florida, succeed in (1) getting the drunken driving on the record, (2) protecting the community even more effectively than would have been accomplished by a weekend jail sentence, and (3) making possible the imposition of potentially rehabilitative conditions such as participation in an alcohol education program.

While the easy communicability, lack of complexity, and potential impact of home confinement as a correctional policy have given it considerable appeal, the greatest advantage in the eyes of many seems to be *reasonable cost*. The examples provided in Chapters 2, 3, and 4 give ample evidence here. Indeed, the search for alternatives to secure, institutional detention or incarceration has probably been driven more in recent years by cost considerations than by any other motive. Those influenced by humanitarian motives may find home confinement appealing as a way of avoiding the brutality of detention facilities, jails, and prisons, and of reducing the stigma with which the offender is branded; but even "get tough" advocates have been forced to consider its use when they are brought face-to-face with the enormous expense of their ideal. Money talks. The authors have been impressed again and again by the fact that participants in any gathering in which the possible implementation of home confinement is being considered, however bored they may be by the alleged humanitarian possibilities, immediately "come alive" when they see comparative cost figures.

To admit this is not to engage in cynicism. The fact is that the state governments grappling with the problem are under heavy financial pressure, while many of the county and municipal governments are in nothing less than a fiscal crisis. One of the major social problems of the 1980s is the need to control costs. Given the size and significance of the federal debt and the movement to reduce revenue-sharing programs by which the federal government has provided assistance to state and local authorities, this problem is likely to grow even more severe. Of course, the savings involved in the use of home confinement will really depend upon the extent to which it is used as an alternative to more expensive alternatives such as secure facilities. If house arrest becomes just one more means of social control, it will simply add to expenses.

Unlike policies requiring increased jail and prison construction, home confinement is characterized by *reversibility*. This is a major policy advantage. Detention facilities, jails, and prisons may be constructed, but if it is later discovered that they are no longer so necessary, given changes in public behavior or perceptions of what is appropriate punishment, the enormous cost will have gone for little or nothing and the taxpayer will be burdened with the added expense of maintenance. Or, as some observers have noted, there may be a pressure to fill the facilities so as to justify their existence. A policy making use of home confinement is quite different. If it is discovered that the practice does not work as envisioned, policy can be reversed with a minimum of expense or administrative disruption. Even in the case of electronic monitoring equipment, the devices seem to pay for themselves in a relatively short time when the policy is vigorously implemented. It is difficult to dismantle a detention facility, jail, or prison that is no longer needed in one location and transport it to another, but such an exchange is quite simple with electronic monitoring equipment.

Still another advantage of home confinement as a correctional policy is its *divisibility*. This makes possible a wide variety of possibilities for structuring periods of confinement. The most obvious possibility is to divide the day into two periods, one for work, school, or other activity considered desirable, and the other for home confinement. But the divisibility of home confinement offers an almost endless set of further possibilities. The policy can be structured, for example, to allow for certain routine absences from the home, such as during a specific block of time set aside for church attendance. In the case of less routine needs, such as medical or dental appointment, permission for exceptions can be obtained in advance.

A few additional examples may make the importance of the divisibility factor even clearer in terms of the alternatives it makes possible. Some judges favor a policy of sentencing certain offenders to serve consecutive weekends in jail, sometimes for as long as a year. The sentence is premised on the idea that the offender will be required to "do the time," but serve the number of jail days while still holding a job. There may be some reluctance to impose such a sentence, however, if the offender is going to be seen on the streets in the meantime, and there is always the chance that he or she will embarrass the court by committing another offense during the interim. The home confinement alternative would allow the judge to set a weekend sentence while adding the condition of home incarceration during specific hours of the day during the week. In this way, the major objective of weekend sentences could be achieved while still keeping the offender "off the streets" during the week.

Some correctional institutions allow "home furloughs" by which, for example, an institutionalized mother may be permitted to leave the facility for a few days to visit her family. Ordinarily, concern over the dangers of releasing to "the streets" too early may delay such furloughs until near the end of the sentence. Home incarceration might allow for more restricted furloughs even earlier, just as it now allows for the increased likelihood of earlier parole given the more intense supervision provided. Many other possibilities will doubtless occur to the reader. The electronic monitoring devices may already be programmed in such a way that the specific confinement schedule for a particular offender may be stored in the computer and changed on a moment's notice so that there may be many different arrangements for required "at home" and permitted "away from home" periods during the day.

In addition to its other advantages, house arrest has the virtue of *compatibility* with existing programs. It would be unrealistic to expect home confinement to represent a viable correctional policy if it were to be seen as in sharp conflict with programs already in place. But this is certainly not the case. There are proponents of jail and prison construction who seem to oppose the concept of home incarceration as a blow to their plans, but it appears to the authors that most of those now involved with the systems of criminal and juvenile justice will find home confinement to be compatible with the programs now in existence.

Not only does home confinement offer a correctional alternative that is compatible with existing programs, but it appears to *facilitate* the actual operation of many of them. As indicated in Chapter 2, the community-based programs for youths, which put heavy emphasis upon keeping them in school and providing them with assistance in the community, can actually be extended to more and more young people with the additional supervision made possible by a home detention program. There is additional evidence that the idea is looked upon with favor by many of those who work with the youths in question because it is perceived as an additional tool that can be of help to them (Huff, 1986). Home confinement offers another tool to the probation officer and another means of supervision to the parole officer. There is the danger that it may force them both into more of a surveillance role with certain offenders, but this may not be of great significance if the alternative is really jail, prison, or even a secure detention facility.

Finally, we would argue that home confinement has the advantage of *perceived relevance to organizational goals* and that this is another feature that may add to the probability of its adoption as an alternative correctional policy. In the case of youth detention, for example, the major organizational goal may be to assure the appearance of the offenders at the place and time required by the court. It would be simple to gain the greatest assurance by locking them in a secure detention facility. But there are other goals as well, including avoiding stigmatization, facilitating schooling and other community-based contributions, and cost containment. All of the latter are better served by a policy of home detention. We have already pointed out some of the ways in which home incarceration can contribute to the realization of organizational goals connected with protecting the public against drunken drivers, and the earlier chapters contain many other examples. Our experience with home confinement under a variety of conditions leads not only to the conclusion that the policy is relevant to the organizational goals of those agencies that may consider it, but also suggest that this relevance is readily perceived.

The many advantages of a house arrest policy has made it more and more popular as a correctional alternative. Indeed, there has been so much euphoria that some consider it almost treason to voice doubts. But no new policy is without its dangers, and it is incumbent upon those who consider a new "alternative" to pay some attention to possible problems. We do not pretend to omniscience; no one is in a position to foresee the future. At the same time, some perspective may be gained if the house arrest movement can be put into historical context, and if consideration can be given to its possible social psychological and political implications.

QUESTIONS AND RESERVATIONS

Our interest in the possibilities of home confinement as an alternative correctional policy was triggered in part by a search for some option to be used in lieu of institutionalization. We were aware that house arrest was nothing new and that some such practices had often been used informally, especially with juveniles. Part of our concern had to do with protecting the due-rocess interests of the offender and providing clearer, formalized policy in order to protect public employees such as probation officers from charges of arbitrary and capricious behavior. The National Advisory Commission on Criminal Justice Standards and Goals for Courts (1973) had made such concerns official, suggesting that a court-approved agreement be required whenever "diversion" involved actual deprivation of liberty, as is the case with the "curfew" or house arrest. Our hope was for (1) formal adoption through enabling legislation and (2) careful evaluation of the policy through systematic research.

It is important to note that while home confinement has been adopted through the legislative process in certain instances, it has been more common to implement it through administrative or judicial fiat. This may pose a problem if only because the policy may be altered with every new administrator or judge. Legislation allows for a full, public debate. This in turn serves to legitimize the practice and to provide for greater consistency in its implementation. As for the "systematic research," quantity is not a substitute for quality. As we pointed out in Chapter 4, the evaluation research, which has attempted to assess the effectiveness of home confinement, has been troubled by many problems, including a lack of random assignment of cases, the necessity of relying upon judges' opinions as to whether, for example, they would have sentenced a given offender to jail had home incarceration not been available as an "alternative," and a host of other difficulties that call its validity into question. This is the product of circumstances rather than the fault of the researchers, but the need for more systematic work is clear.

Many of the potential legal and administrative issues have already been addressed in earlier chapters. Because of our conviction that home confinement should be advanced through the legislative process, we have included examples in the appendices. At some point, when the policy has developed a "track record" and its implications are clearer, there will be a need for model legislation. Meanwhile, such examples may be of assistance. For similar reasons, we have provided samples of supervision contracts, reporting forms, and other administrative materials that may serve as examples of the way "house arrest" policy can be implemented in a more systematic and professional fashion to the benefit of both offenders and those charged with their supervision.

Beyond these issues are others more difficult to address. As Marx (1981: 242) has shown in his analysis of the "ironies" of social control, "It would appear that modern society increasingly generates ironic outcomes, whether iatrogenic effects . . . unintended consequences of new technologies . . . or the familiar sociological examples found in prisons and mental hospitals or in the careers of urban renewal and various other efforts at social reform." These "ironic outcomes" frequently mean that a "solution" to one problem creates one or more new problems that may be worse. To anticipate this sort of thing might be considered mere paranoia if it were not so clear that the tendency is built into the system, including the increasing complexity and interdependence of social life and the increased effort at intervention based upon expansion of professionalism and expertise (Marx, 1981). This may be the case with house arrest, and there is an obligation to confront the possibility.

Although home confinement is still insufficiently developed as a formal correctional policy to allow for any early predictions, some trends seem to give reason to wonder about the future. In our earliest work with home incarceration, for example, we advocated the use of volunteers to assist with the monitoring of compliance (Ball and Lilly, 1983a). The practical reason for this was to reduce pressures on probation officers. More generally, however, the suggestion was argued in terms of our theoretical perspective, which seeks to facilitate the reconciliation of offender and community. Given monitoring by volunteers, the offender would be involved with representatives of the local community rather than with government officials, and it was hoped that the use of volunteers would contribute to the increased involvement of the public in the systems of criminal and juvenile justice. Given what seemed to be both practical and theoretical advantages of the use of community volunteers to monitor compliance, it is important to consider the extent to which the actual implementation of this alternative has been accomplished through the much more expensive and much less communal option of electronic monitoring.

The fact is that new correctional policies are rarely carried out as originally envisioned. They tend to be caught in a common pattern involving a "dialectics of reform," in which the established agents of social control who operate the criminal and juvenile justice systems on a day-to-day basis accept certain "reforms," but only on their own terms (Austin and Krisberg, 1981). Despite our theoretical position stressing the reconciliation of offender and community, we were troubled from the beginning by evidence that suggested that the "community" might actually resist such reconciliation (Greenberg, 1975). The eagerness to embrace electronic monitoring now suggests that those operating the criminal and juvenile justice systems may be more interested in maintaining tight, bureaucratic control over offenders than in opening supervision programs to the public. Of course, it must be admitted that the electronic monitoring is likely to be a more reliable system, freer from problems of "human error." Whether this is good or bad depends upon one's point of view.

We have already touched upon some of the major concerns troubling some of those engaged in experimentation with home confinement in the examination of social issues of privacy in Chapter 5. The sociohistorical and social psychological problems here are quite complex. We cannot go as far as the National Advisory Commission on Criminal Justice Standards and Goals for Corrections (1973: 222) in assuming that "the humanitarian aspect of community-based corrections is obvious." The use of the home as a jail, prison, or detention facility may contribute to the further blurring of the old distinction between what is public and what is private. As Hylton (1982) has pointed out, the President's Commission (1967) recognized years ago that any such blurring of lines between institutional treatment and community treatment might affect the rights of offenders. To what extent may it also affect the very concept of individuality?

As we indicated in Chapter 1, one's interpretation of the trend toward increased use of house arrest will be conditioned by one's reading of the history of correctional policy. Is it essentially a history of progress? Is it better interpreted as a history of unintended consequences and unfortunate "ironies?" Or is it really a history of the extension of total control over the individual? If the pattern is one of "progress," then it may be reasonable to accept house arrest as a continuation of correctional policy into more and more progressive and "civilized" practices. If the pattern is one of good ideas going wrong or leading to unforeseen and unfortunate consequences, it becomes especially important that those implementing house arrest do so with special caution and change course quickly if things begin to go wrong. If it is more accurately interpreted as a pattern of historical extension of control over the individual, the danger that house arrest is part of a larger trend that may lead toward the extinction of individuality is very real.

We will make no attempt to deal with these issues here. Indeed, any such effort may be largely speculative, and we regard the present volume as an introduction to the current policy and practice of house arrest rather than as an intensive critique. We would be less than honest, however, if we did not admit to being troubled by the two trends mentioned in Chapter 1, the proliferation of technology and the recent changes in the political climate. The future of both developments is difficult to predict, but both may have enormous impact upon the future of house arrest. Put briefly, the growth of technology is placing more and more power in the hands of those who control it. The question is: How will it be used?

As indicated in Chapter 1, the shift in the political climate that occurred in the late 1970s and continued into the 1980s seems to have represented a backlash against much of what had happened in the 1960s, including the work of the Warren Court, which had extended the rights of the individual at the expense of the power of the state. Had house arrest come on the scene in the 1960s, at a time when concern for individual rights was running high and the Supreme Court, for example, was handing down rulings that actually extended the right to privacy, there might have been less reason for concern. But the recent political climate is much different.

Two of the most obvious examples of the shift in the political climate in the 1980s are found in the intense interest of the government in drugs and sex. In both cases it has been argued that these are "private matters," which, when criminalized, amount to "victimless crimes," whereby the offender may be using his or her body in a way that has been declared illegal by the state, but is either "hurting no one" or, at least, "no one else." It is not our intention to argue for or against the morality of such activities. Nor do we take a position with respect to whether the state ought to intervene in attempts to control them through the power of the criminal justice system. Our point is simply that a distinct political shift has occurred here, one that has implications for the future of house arrest.

The shift in the political climate has made definitions of *privacy* unstable, especially when either drugs or sex are involved. In 1986, Congress made an $11.7 billion budget cut, a move that reduced the budget of the U.S. Department of Justice by approximately 4.3% (*Criminal Justice Newsletter*, 1986a, 1986b). During the early summer of 1986 the Department of Justice had to suspend jury trials because it did not have the funds to pay jurors the required $30 per day per diem (*Criminal Justice Newsletter*, 1986b). Yet shortly afterward the federal government declared a new $250 million "war on drugs" (*Newsweek*, 1986; *Time*, 1986). This "war" was to extend the recent use of drug testing of employees in the world of business and athletics to federal employees, despite the lack of any evidence that those to be tested had used illegal drugs or had committed any crime at all. And the announcement came after a five-month Congressional study that concluded that "urinalysis procedures are expensive, 'useless in most cases,' and often inaccurate" (*Washington Post*, 1986: 15). The federal government was described as in a "frenzy" over drugs (*New York Times*, 1986: 25). Despite arguments that what employees do on their "private time" is their "own business" unless it affects job performance, and that such testing replaces the due-process assumption of innocence with a crime control assumption of guilt until proven otherwise, a White House poll was able to report that "the public is more worried about drugs than about such matters as the federal budget deficit and arms control" (*Time*, August 18, 1986: 12), the implication being that the "rights of society" override those of the individual in such cases.

With respect to sexual activity, the political shift is almost equally obvious. The early 1980s saw many efforts to overturn the Supreme

Court decision in *Roe v. Wade* (1973), which had struck down statutes limiting abortions. The decision in *Roe v. Wade* has rested to a considerable extent upon the Court's judgment that state interests were not compelling enough to justify such interference in the personal privacy of women as the particular legislation in question allowed. The more recent arguments contend that the interests of the state in maintaining public morality are more than sufficient to justify the criminalization of abortion. Similar arguments have been made as to the right of the state to restrict and monitor the activities of AIDS victims, the arguments here focusing upon the right of the government to restrict individual liberty in the interest of public protection.

Also, in the summer of 1986, came a public outcry over a Supreme Court decision in *Bowers v. Hardwick* (1986), a decision that upheld the sodomy law of Georgia. In this case, by the narrowest possible margin (5-4), the Court upheld a Georgia law that makes it a felony, punishable by 20 years in prison, for consenting adults to engage in oral or anal sexual relations. The case developed innocently enough as a police officer went to Hardwick's apartment to serve a warrant for carrying an open container of alcohol in a public place. The officer was ushered into the apartment by a guest and told that Hardwick could be found in his bedroom. There the officer discovered Hardwick engaged in oral sex with another man and made an arrest. The case was not prosecuted, but Hardwick himself challenged the arrest. In effect, the Court ruled that individuals under Georgia law had no right to engage in such acts even as consenting adults in a private bedroom, taking the position that the state had a legitimate right to restrict and control these activities as part of its responsibilities for enforcing public morality even in private places.

Given the shift in the political climate and the underlying legal and social disagreements as to the meaning and value of privacy, the house arrest movement becomes very difficult to interpret. It may represent another step in historical progress, a "humanitarian" alternative to secure detention, jail, or prison. On the other hand, it may turn out to have some unanticipated consequences of a very unfortunate sort. It is even possible that some of the more severe critics are right and that house arrest is one more step toward the total control of the citizenry. As we have indicated elsewhere, house arrest of youths who otherwise quite clearly would have been institutional- ized in secure detention facilities is a different thing from house arrest, involving electronic monitoring of adults who might well have been released on their own recognizance, had the more restrictive "alternative" been unavailable. Much will depend upon the extent to which the "net is widened," and much will depend upon the extent to which due process is guaranteed. The legal issues may turn out to be more complex than expected. The broader social issues demand debate, especially if house arrest is extended to embrace more and more offenders.

APPENDIX A
Court Order for House Arrest,
Jefferson County (Kentucky) Juvenile Court

HOUSE ARREST

Rather than being placed in the Jefferson County Youth Center pending your next appearance in Court, the Judge is allowing you to live at home under certain conditions. It must be understood that you are in detention and under the supervision of the Court, just as if you were in the Youth Center, except that the Judge has allowed you to be in detention at home rather than in the Youth Center.

You must remain at home at all times except for certain situations listed below. You may go outside your house, but must remain on your own property. You are not to visit with any of your friends or associates at any time, and they may not visit you.

The exceptions are as follows:

1) You may travel directly to school or work and directly home from school or work; however, this must be done without delay of any kind.

2) You may travel directly to and from the Juvenile Court or the Youth Center for the purpose of keeping appointments set by the Court.

3) You may travel directly to and from religious services. Again, this is without any delay of any kind.

4) You are not to leave your home on any other occasion except in the company of a parent or legal guardian, and then only for important reasons such as necessary shopping, visiting a sick relative, attending a funeral, or keeping medical appointments.

If you violate this order and are apprehended you will automatically spend the remainder of the time in the Youth Center.

It is the responsibility of your parent, legal guardian, or other person to whom you have been released to enforce this rule. If you violate the rules of house arrest it is their responsibility to immediately notify the Court of this violation.

If you violate these rules and your parent or guardian does not immediately contact the Court, then they can be prosecuted for contempt of Court or for contributing to the delinquency of a minor.

No exception is to be made to the above rules:

JUDGE
JEFFERSON COUNTY JUVENILE COURT

Home Supervision Contract,
Jefferson County (Kentucky) Juvenile Court

HOME SUPERVISION CONTRACT

DATE:_____

NAME:_____

CASE NO._____

The following conditions are designed to keep the Home Supervision referral trouble free while before the Court, and not as a punishment for any alleged offense.

I, the undersigned, agree to abide by these conditions in order to reside at home instead of the Jefferson County Youth Center while before the Court.

1. I understand and agree to obey my parents and/or guardians and the rules of the house.

2. I will maintain a daily curfew of _____ and a weekend curfew of _____.

3. I will not be out of the house unless given permission by my parents or guardian, in which case I will keep them informed of my whereabouts at all times, to include names, address, phone numbers, etc.

4. I understand I must appear in Juvenile Court on the appointed dates and times.

5. I understand and agree to keep all appointments with my worker, also appointments made for me with others.

6. If I am of the mandatory school age, I understand and agree to be enrolled and in daily attendance in a school and not cause trouble.

7. If I am over the mandatory school age, I am willing to seek employment.

8. Special Agreements:_____
    _____
    _____
    _____
    _____

I understand that if I violate any of these conditions, I will be returned to Court for further restrictions.

Date:_____   Signed: _____

Witnessed by: _____
              Parents/Guardian

_____
Worker

APPENDIX C
Cuyahoga County (Ohio) Juvenile
Court Home Detention Order (Contract)

COUNTY OF
CUYAHOGA

Juvenile Detention Center
2209 Central Avenue / Cleveland, Ohio 44115

JUVENILE COURT
HOME DETENTION ORDER

In the interest of _____
A child under 18 years of age.

RULES OF SUPERVISION

You have been placed by the Court under the Supervision of the Home Detention Unit of the Juvenile Court. This means that the Court believes you, with the help and support of your parents and the Home Detention Worker, can be a responsible citizen pending your scheduled Court Hearing.

The Court requires that you live within the general and special rules of supervision which are listed on the following pages. If you fail to abide by any of these rules, it may be necessary for the Court to return you to the custody of the Superintendent, Juvenile Detention Center, pending your court hearing.

HOME DETENTION ORDER

I, _____ , will obey the rules of this Home Detention Order that are checked on the following pages, I further agree to obey the laws of this community, keep appointments on time, and cooperate with my parent(s) and Home Detention worker, as part of this order. I understand that breaking any of these rules could cause me to return to the Juvenile Detention Center.

(continued)

RESIDENCE

[   ] 1. I will remain at my place of residence at all times of the day and night.

[   ] 2. I will leave my residence only during school hours, _____ to _____ , and come directly home after school.

[   ] 3. I will leave my residence only during work hours, _____ to _____ , and come directly home after work.

[   ] 4. I will leave my residence only when my parent(s) or Home Detention worker is with me.

[   ] 5. I will leave my residence only on weekends and only with the permission of my parents and Home Detention worker.

[   ] 6. I will leave my place of residence only with the permission of my parent(s) and Home Detention worker.

[   ] 7. I will notify my Home Detention worker of any change of address.

HOURS

[   ] 8. I will obey the hours set for me on a daily basis by my parent(s) and Home Detention worker.

[   ] 9. If given the permission of my parent(s) and Home Detention worker to leave my residence, I will return to my residence no later than the following curfew:
Sunday through Thursday _____
Friday and Saturday _____

SCHOOL/WORK

[   ] 10. I will attend school and all my classes regularly, unless my parent(s) and Home Detention worker give me permission to remain at home.

[   ] 11. I will have school slips signed daily and turn them in to my Home Detention worker. I will obey the school rules and regulations.

[   ] 12. I will be at work every day unless my parent(s) and Home Detention worker give me permission to remain at home.

DRIVING

[   ] 13. I will not drive a car or other motorized vehicle.

[   ] 14. I will drive a car or other motorized vehicle only when my parent(s) or Home Detention worker is with me.

[   ] 15. I will drive a car or other motorized vehicle only when given permission by my parent(s) and Home Detention worker.

(continued)

ACTIVITIES

[ ] 16. I will participate in activities with other persons only if given prior permission by my parent(s) and Home Detention worker.

[ ] 17. I will not associate with persons whom my parent(s) and Home Detention worker prohibit me from seeing.

[ ] 18. Specifically, I will not associate with the following persons:

SPECIAL RULES

[ ] 19. As part of this order, I will obey the following conditions:

_____

_____

_____

_____

_____

_____

The order will be in effect until your Court hearing.

Place of residence: _____

_____   _____
Juvenile   Date   Home Detention Project Director   Date

As the parent/guardian, I understand the   The Home Detention worker assigned to this
conditions of this order and agree to actively   case is:
participate in and support its enforcement
with the assistance of the Home Detention
Worker.   Name: _____

                                                Phone: _____
_____
Parent(s)/Guardian   Date

Cuyahoga County Home Detention Project Daily Contact Log

Home Detention
Daily Contact Log

Child's Name _____

Home Detention
Worker's Name _____

Date	Contact	Time Start	Time Finish	Child's Signature/Comments
	Child			
	School visit			
	Home visit			
	Parent contact			
	Collateral contact			
	Child			
	School visit			
	Home visit			
	Parent contact			
	Collateral contact			
	Child			
	School visit			
	Home visit			
	Parent contact			
	Collateral contact			
	Child			
	School visit			
	Home visit			
	Parent contact			
	Collateral contact			
	Child			
	School visit			
	Home visit			
	Parent contact			
	Collateral contact			
	Child			
	School visit			
	Home visit			
	Parent contact			
	Collateral contact			
	Child			
	School visit			
	Home visit			
	Parent contact			
	Collateral contact			
	Child			
	School visit			
	Home visit			
	Parent contact			
	Collateral contact			
	Child			
	School visit			
	Home visit			
	Parent contact			

APPENDIX E
Cuyahoga County Home Detention Project School Report Form

COURT OF COMMON PLEAS

JUVENILE COURT DIVISION

KENNETH A. ROCCO
Administrative Judge

Judges
JOHN J. TONER
JOHN F. CORRIGAN
LEODIS HARRIS
BETTY WILLIS RUBEN

ALLYN R. SIELAFF
Court Administrator

RONALD STEPANIK
Superintendent
Detention Center

DETENTION CENTER
COUNTY OF CUYAHOGA
2209 CENTRAL AVENUE
CLEVELAND, OHIO 44115

(216) 443 3300

HOME DETENTION PROJECT

SCHOOL REPORT FORM

Pupil Name _____ HR _____ DATE _____

	Class/Teacher/Subject	Days Abs.	Grade	Behavior/Comments
1.				
2.				
3.				
4.				
5.				
6.				
7.				
8.				

Home Room Teacher
Remarks ___ _____

Home Detention Worker

_____

Phone Number

157

APPENDIX F
Cuyahoga County Home Detention Project Violation Report Form

HOME DETENTION VIOLATION REPORT

Child's Name: _____

Date of Referral: _____

Date of Return: _____

Summary of Child's Behavior:

_____
HOME DETENTION WORKER

Remember to turn in Data Slip and close off Master.

HOME DETENTION VIOLATION REPORT

Child's Name: _____

Date of Referral: _____

Date of Return: _____

Summary of Child's Behavior:

_____
HOME DETENTION WORKER

Remember to turn in Datea Slip and close off Master.

JC78006 (X)

APPENDIX G
Cuyahoga County Home Detention Project
Home Detention Report (Final Report to Court)

HOME DETENTION REPORT

Child's Name _____

Home Detention
Worker's Name _____

Dates on Home Detention: From _____ to _____

Number of Personal Contacts _____ Number of Phone Contacts _____ School Contacts _____

Comments _____

Family Relationships (Family composition, functioning of family members towards one another).
_____
_____
_____
_____
_____
_____
_____
_____
_____

Home Environment: (a brief description of the home, and the neighborhood). _____
_____
_____
_____

School Situation: Name of School _____ Grade _____

Attitude and Behavior _____
_____
_____
_____

Attendance: _____

Summary of child's behavior on Home Detention. _____
_____
_____
_____
_____

Evaluation: _____
_____
_____
_____

Date of Report: _____   Submitted by: _____

Kentucky Revised Statute 532: 200-250

HOME INCARCERATION

532.200 Definitions

As used in KRS 532.210 to 532.250, unless the context otherwise requires:

(1) "Home" means the temporary or permanent residence of a defendant consisting of the actual living area. Where more than one (1) residence or family is located on a single piece of property, "home" does not include the residence of any other person who is not part of the social unit formed by the defendant's immediate family. A hospital, nursing care facility, hospice, half-way house, group home, residential treatment facility or boarding house may serve as a "home" under this section;

(2) "Home incarceration" means use of a person's home for purposes of confinement;

(3) "Violent felony offense" means an offense defined in KRS 507.020 (murder), 507.030 (manslaughter in the first degree), 508.010 (assault in the first degree), 508.020 (assault in the second degree), 509.040 (kidnapping), 510.040 (rape in the first degree), 510.070 (sodomy in the first degree), 510.110 (sexual abuse in the first degree), 511.020 (burglary in the first degree), 513.020 (arson in the first degree), 513.030 (arson in the second degree), 513.040 (arson in the third degree), 515.020 (robbery in the first degree), 515.030 (robbery in the second degree), 520.020 (escape in the first degree), any criminal attempt to commit any such offense (KRS 506.010), or conviction as a persistent felony offender (KRS 532.080) when the offender has a felony conviction for any of the above-listed offenses within the five (5) year period preceding the date of the latest conviction;

(4) "Terminal illness" is a medically recognized disease for which the prognosis is death within six (6) months to a reasonable degree of medical certainty; and

(5) "Approved monitoring device" means an electronic device approved by the corrections cabinet or apparatus which is limited in capability to recording or transmitting information as to the prisoner's presence or non-presence in the home. Such devices must be minimally intrusive. No monitoring device capable of recording or transmitting:

(a) Visual images;

(b) Oral or wire communications or any auditory sound; or

(c) Information as to the prisoner's activities while inside the home;
shall be approved.

HISTORY: 1986 c 243, § 1, eff. 7-15-86

532.210 Petition; study of record; order

(1) Any misdemeanant may petition the sentencing court for an order directing that all or a portion of a sentence of imprisonment in the county jail be served under conditions of home incarceration. Such petitions may be considered and ruled upon by the sentencing court prior to and throughout the term of the misdemeanant's sentence.

(2) The sentencing judge shall study the record of all persons petitioning for home incarceration and, in his discretion, may:

(a) Cause additional background or character information to be collected or reduced to writing by the county jailer or misdemeanor supervision department;

(b) Conduct hearings on the desirability of granting home incarceration;

(c) Impose on the home incarceree such conditions as are fit, including restitution;

(continued)

APPENDIX H Continued

(d) Order that all or a portion of a sentence of imprisonment in the county jail be served under conditions of home incarceration at whatever time or intervals, consecutive or non-consecutive, as the court shall determine. The time actually spent in home incarceration pursuant to this provision shall not exceed six (6) months or the maximum term of imprisonment assessed pursuant to this chapter whichever is the shorter;

(e) Issue warrants for persons when there is reason to believe they have violated the conditions of home incarceration, conduct hearings on such matters, and order reimprisonment in the county jail upon proof of violation; and

(f) Grant final discharge from incarceration.

(3) All home incarcerees shall execute a written agreement with the court setting forth all of the conditions of home incarceration. The order of home incarceration shall incorporate that agreement and order compliance with its terms. The order and agreement shall be transmitted to the supervising authority and to the appropriate jail official.

(4) Time spent in home incarceration under this subsection shall be credited against the maximum term of imprisonment assessed for the defendant pursuant to this chapter.

(5) Home incarcerees shall be under the supervision of the county jailer except in counties establishing misdemeanor supervision departments, wherein they shall be under the supervision of such departments. Home incarcerees shall be subject to the decisions of such authorities during the period of supervision. Fees for supervision or equipment usage shall be paid directly to the supervising authority.

HISTORY: 1986 c 243, § 2, eff. 7-15-86

532.220 Conditions

The conditions of home incarceration shall include the following:

(1) The home incarceree shall be confined to his home at all times except when:

(a) Working at approved employment or traveling directly to and from such employment;

(b) Seeking employment;

(c) Undergoing available medical, psychiatric, or mental health treatment or approved counseling and after care programs;

(d) Attending an approved educational institution or program;

(e) Attending a regularly scheduled religious service at a place of worship; and

(f) Participating in an approved community work service program;

(2) Violation of subsection (1) of this section may subject the home incarceree to prosecution under KRS 520.030 (escape);

(3) The home incarceree shall conform to a schedule prepared by a designated officer of the supervising authority specifically setting forth the times when he may be absent from the home and the locations where he may be during those times;

(4) The home incarceree shall not commit another offense during the period of time for which he is subject to the conditions of home incarceration;

(5) The home incarceree shall not change the place of home incarceration or the schedule without prior approval of the supervising authority;

(6) The home incarceree shall maintain a telephone or other approved monitoring device in the home or on his person at all times;

(continued)

APPENDIX H Continued

(7) Any other reasonable conditions set by the court or the supervising authority including:
(a) Restitution under KRS 533.030;
(b) Supervision fees under KRS 439.315; and
(c) Any of the conditions imposed on persons on probation or conditional discharge under KRS 533.030(2); and
(8) A written and notarized consent agreement shall be filed with the court by every adult who will share the offender's home during the term of home incarceration.

HISTORY: 1986 c 243, § 3, eff. 7-15-86

532.230 Ineligibility

No person being held under a detainer, warrant, or process issued by some other jurisdiction shall be eligible for home incarceration. No person convicted of a violent felony offense shall be eligible for home incarceration.

HISTORY: 1986 c 243, § 4, eff. 7-15-86

532.240 Responsibilities of persons held in home incarceration

Any person serving his sentence under conditions of home incarceration shall be responsible for his food, housing, clothing, and medical care expenses, and shall be eligible for government benefits to the same extent as a person on probation, parole, or conditional discharge.

HISTORY: 1986 c 243, § 5, eff. 7-15-86

532.250 Monthly list of incarcerees provided to local law enforcement agencies

At least once every thirty (30) days, the supervising authority shall provide all local and county law enforcement agencies with a list of the offenders under home incarceration in their jurisdictions. This list shall include the following information:

(1) The prisoner's place of home incarceration;
(2) The crime for which the prisoner was convicted;
(3) The date that the sentence of home incarceration will be completed; and
(4) The name, address and phone number of the officer of the authority supervising the prisoner.

HISTORY: 1986 c 243, § 6, eff. 7-15-86

APPENDIX I
Presentence Investigation Report: Kentucky

JC-107-10-038E

SOURCE OF INFORMATION SHEET

(PRESENTENCE INVESTIGATION REPORT)

MEMO

TO: District Supervisor

FROM:

RE: _____, Client

DATE COMPLETED:

In completing this investigation, I have contacted the following persons and agencies for verification and information:

OFFENSE (OFFICIAL VERSION):

Name or Agency	Title	Date	Type of Contact

PRIOR RECORD:

Source	Address	Date

EDUCATION - EMPLOYMENT:

Name	School or Company	Date	Type of Contact

Referral for Presentence Interview (Home Incarceration)

COMMONWEALTH OF KENTUCKY
SIXTEENTH JUDICIAL DISTRICT
KENTON DISTRICT COURT

COMMONWEALTH OF KENTUCKY   PLAINTIFF

VS.   REFERRAL FOR PRESENTENCE INTERVIEW   NO._____
                              (HOME INCARCERATION)

_____   DEFENDANT

                              * * *

      The abovenamed defendant has pled guilty or been convicted of

_____, in violation of

KRS _____.

      The defendant shall report to the Office of Probation and Parole,

Room 706, Covington/Kenton County Building, on Wednesday, _____, 19___,

at 1:00 p.m. for a Presentence Interview to determine whether or not this

defendant would be appropriate for probation on terms of Home Incarceration.

      The defendant shall appear to be sentenced on this charge on

_____, 19___, in Courtroom ____, Covington/Kenton County Building,

at _____ a.m./p.m.

      The office of Probation and Parole is requested to conduct the

Presentence Interview and make report to the Court prior to the sentencing

hearing.

                              KENTON DISTRICT COURT

(continued)

APPENDIX J Continued

JC-107-10-038E
BRIEF NARRATIVE ON CHILDHOOD, ETC. - MARITAL HISTORY AND NARRATIVE:

Name or Agency   Relationship   Date   Type of Contact

_____

_____

_____

_____

_____

_____

COMMUNITY AND OFFICIAL ATTITUDE:

Name   Relationship   Address   Type of Contact

_____

_____

_____

_____

_____

_____

OUT OF DISTRICT CASE:

To complete the out-of-district investigation I have made a written
request for information from:

State or District _____   Date _____

_____

_____

_____

INSTRUCTIONS:

Complete one copy of this form on each presentence investigation made. Officers on
probationary status will submit the form attached to the presentence investigation
report to the supervisor. Officers on permanent status will complete the form and
retain in the client's file.

Type of contact should be listed as: office, telephone, home, community, etc.

This report need not be typed.

APPENDIX K
Kenton County, Kentucky, House Arrest Monitor Form

```
                        KENTON COUNTY
                    HOUSE ARREST MONITOR

BAND #:          SS #:     -  -      CASE #:              FILE #:

First Name:                    Middle Initial:    Last Name:

Address:                          Apt. #:
City:                        State: KY   Zip:              Phone:

DOB:   /  /   Sex:    Race:    Eyes:    Hair:    Hgt:       Wgt:
BEGIN DATE:    /  /       CLIENT STATUS:      END DATE:    /  /
COMMENTS:

DAY   START TIME 1   STOP TIME 1   START TIME 2   STOP TIME 2
MON
TUE
WED
THU
FRI
SAT
SUN
```

APPENDIX L
Position of the Unitarian Universalist Service Committee National Moratorium on Prison Construction: Electronic Home Incarceration

 Unitarian Universalist Service Committee
National Moratorium on Prison Construction

309 Pennsylvania Ave SE Washington DC 20003 (202) 547-3633

POSITION OF THE UNITARIAN UNIVERSALIST SERVICE COMMITTEE NATIONAL MORATORIUM ON PRISON CONSTRUCTION: ELECTRONIC HOME INCARCERATION

Since its first public use in 1983, electronically monitored home incarceration has become a rapidly expanding new field of criminal justice. Pretrial, probation and parole authorities around the nation are investigating and experimenting with electronic devices that allow an individual to be monitored at a fixed location, the home, under conditions of house arrest. The Unitarian Universalist Service Committee National Moratorium on Prison Construction opposes current use of this electronic surveillance technology and holds that it should not be viewed as an alternative to incarceration or future prison construction for these reasons:

1) Electronic house arrest is not being used as an alternative to incarceration, but is instead becoming a new sanction for low-risk and minor offenders who would not otherwise be incarcerated. In jurisdictions where new categories of minor offenders are being imprisoned under mandatory sentencing laws, it is inappropriate to usher in electronic surveillance as a necessary "alternative" to overcrowded prisons.

2) The use of electronic surveillance technology to monitor citizens in their homes raises political, civil and human rights questions that go far beyond the criminal justice system. Until these issues come to the forefront of debate and are resolved, further advances in electronic home incarceration threaten to undermine these rights.

3) Current innovations in electronic monitoring systems indicate that the lines between various surveillance functions (e.g., fixed location monitoring, audio, visual, tracking) are being blurred. Without consensus on what forms of electronic monitoring are acceptable or overly intrusive, we are likely to see the application and establishment of many new types of monitoring.

October, 1986

UUSC HEADQUARTERS
78 Beacon Street
Boston, MA 02108
(617) 742-2120

NMPC SAN FRANCISCO
2519 Mission Street
Suite 3
San Francisco, CA 94110
(415) 647-1890

ADVISORY PANEL
Hon. Margaret Burnham
Leonel J. Castillo
Dr. Julius Debro
Prof. M. Kay Harris
Rev. Virginia Mackey
William Marsh
Elizabeth Martinez

Dr. Garry Mendez
William G. Nagel
Mary Ann B. Oakley
Trinidad Sanchez S.J.
Dr. Lawrence Trujillo
Leonard Weinglass
Stanley Wise

References

AARONSON, DAVID E., B. H. HOFF, P. JASZI, N. KITTRIE, and D. SARRI (1977) The New Justice: Alternatives to Conventional Criminal Adjudication. Washington, DC: Government Printing Office.

ALLEN, HARRY E. and CLIFFORD E. SIMONSEN (1986) Corrections in America. New York: Macmillan.

Alliance for Cooperative Justice (1986) Personal correspondence (March).

ALTMAN, IRWIN (1974) "Privacy: A conceptual analysis," in D. H. Carson (ed.) Man-Environment Interactions: Evaluations and Applications. Washington, DC: Environmental Design Research Association.

American Bar Association/Institute of Judicial Administration (1980) Standards. New York: American Bar Association.

ANDREWS, W. (1890) Old-Time Punishments. London: Hull.

AUSTIN, J. and B. KRISBERG (1981) "Wider, stronger and different nets: The dialectics of criminal justice reform." Journal of Research in Crime and Delinquency 18: 165-196.

BALL, DONALD (1968) "Toward a sociology of telephones and telephoners," in M. Truzzi (ed.) Sociology and Everyday Life. Englewood Cliffs, NJ: Prentice-Hall.

BALL, RICHARD A. and J. ROBERT LILLY (1983a) "Home incarceration: An alternative to total incarceration." Presented at IX International Congress on Criminology, Vienna.

BALL, RICHARD A. and J. ROBERT LILLY (1983b) "The potential use of home incarceration with drunken drivers." Presented at meetings of the American Society of Criminology, San Francisco.

BALL, RICHARD A. and J. ROBERT LILLY (1984a) "Theoretical examination of home incarceration." Presented at meetings of the American Society of Criminology, Cincinnati.

BALL, RICHARD A. and J. ROBERT LILLY (1984b) "Giving birth to electronic shackles in Kentucky." Presented at meetings of the American Society of Criminology, Cincinnati.

BALL, RICHARD A. and J. ROBERT LILLY (1985) "Home incarceration: An international alternative to institutional incarceration." International Journal of Comparative and Applied Criminal Justice 9: 85-97.

BALL, RICHARD A. and J. ROBERT LILLY (1986a). "The potential use of home incarceration with drunken drivers." Crime and Delinquency 32: 224-247.

BALL, RICHARD A. and J. ROBERT LILLY (1986b) "A theoretical examination of home incarceration." Federal Probation 50: 17-24.

BALL, RICHARD A. and J. ROBERT LILLY (1988) "The Phenomenology of Privacy and the Power of Electronic Monitoring," in Joseph E. Scott and Travis Hirschi (eds.) Critical Issues in Criminology and Criminal Justice. Newbury Park, CA: Sage.

BARNES (1969) The Repression of Crime: Studies in Historical Penology. Montclair, NJ: Patterson Smith.

BEAUMONT, GUSTAVE de and ALEXIS de TOCQUEVILLE (1964) On the Penetentiary System in the United States and Its Applicability to France (Francis Lieber, trans.) (1833). Carbondale: Southern Illinois University Press.

BECK, ALLEN J. and L. A. GREENFIELD (1985) "Prisoners in 1984." Bureau of Justice Statistics Bulletin. U.S. Department of Justice.

BERRY, BONNIE (1985) "Electronic jails: A new criminal justice concern." Justice Quarterly 2: 1-22.

BILLITTERI, THOMAS J. (1986) "Public companies: A changing cast of characters." Florida Trends (July): 65.

BLOUSTEIN, EDWARD (1964) "Privacy as an aspect of human dignity: An answer to Dean Prosser." New York University Law Review 39: 962-1007.

BOWKER, LEE H. (1982) Corrections: The Science and the Art. New York: Macmillan.

BRECKRENRIDGE, ADAM C. (1970) The Right to Privacy. Lincoln: University of Nebraska Press.

BROWN, JENEE W., ROBERT E. SHEPHERD, Jr., and ANDREW SHOOKHOFF (1985) Preventive Detention after Schall v. Martin. Washington, DC: American Bar Association.

BROWN, KENNETH W. (1986) Re: Corrections Services, Inc (CSI) Research report. Boca Raton, FL: Brown & Hawk, Inc.

Center for the Study of Youth Policy (1986) The Incarceration of Minority Youth. Minneapolis: Hubert Humphrey Institute of Public Affairs, University of Minnesota. (unpublished)

Cincinnati Enquirer (1985) "Kenton OKs 'in-home' jail: Florida judge applauds." January 18: C-2.

COHEN, S. (1985) Visions of Social Control. Cambridge, England: Polity Press.

Community Research Center (1980) An Assessment of the National Incidence of Juvenile Suicide in Adult Jails, Lockups, and Juvenile Detention Centers. Champaign, IL: Community Research Center.

CORBETT, RONALD P. and ELLSWORTH A.L. FERSCH (1985) "Home as prison: The use of house arrest." Federal Probation 49: 13-17.

Corrections Magazine (1983) "Probation 'bracelets': The Spiderman solution." 9: 4.

CORY, BRUCE and STEPHEN GETTINGER (1984) Time to Build? The Realities of Prison Construction. Edna McConnel Clark Foundation.

Criminal Justice Newsletter (1983) "Computerized cuffs come of age." Vol. 14, No. 7 (March 1): 4.

Criminal Justice Newsletter (1985a) "Federal judge, citing costs of prison, imposes 'house arrest.'" Vol. 16, No. 19 (October 1): 2-3.

Criminal Justice Newsletter (1985b) "Electronic monitoring of probationers on the increase." Vol. 16, No. 20 (October 15): 4-6.

Criminal Justice Newsletter (1986a) "Federal judge says courts cannot absorb Gramm-Rudman Act." Vol. 17, No. 7 (April 1): 5-6.

Criminal Justice Newsletter (1986b) "Current budget cuts maintained despite ruling on deficit law." Vol. 17, No. 14 (July 15): 1-2.

DASH, SAMUEL, RICHARD F. SCHWARTZ, and ROBERT E. KNOWLTON (1959) The Eavesdroppers. New York: DeCapo.

DEL CARMEN, ROLANDO V. and JOSEPH VAUGHN (1986) "Legal issues in the use of electronic surveillance in probation." Federal Probation 50: 130-142.

DEL CARMEN, ROLANDO V. (1982) Potential Liabilities of Probation and Parole Officers. Washington, DC: National Institute of Corrections.

DICKENS, CHARLES (1848) Dombey and Son. London: Bradbury & Evan.

DICKENS, CHARLES (1861) Great Expectations. London: Chapman and Hall.

DIONISOPOULOS, P. ALLAN and CRAIG R. DUCAT (1976) The Right to Privacy: Essays and Cases. St. Paul, MN: West.

DRYDEN, JOHN (1669) The Wild Gallant. London: H. Heringman.

Electronics Week (1985) "High-tech leg irons put to the test." March 4: 30.

EMERSON, RALPH WALDO (1856) English Traits. Boston: Phillips, Samson.

Evening Times [Palm Beach] (1984) "A Way to Make Society Safer?" Nov. 29.

Federal Register (1986) "Parolling, recommitting and supervising federal prisoners." Vol. 50, No. 50 (March): 8903-8904.

FISCHER, C. T. (1975) "Privacy as a profile of authentic consciousness." Humanitas 11: 27-44.

FLYNN, LEONARD E. (1986) "House arrest: Florida's alternative eases crowding and tight budgets." Corrections Today (July): 64-68.

FORD, D. and A. SCHMIDT (1985) Electronically monitored home confinement. NIJ Reports (November): 2-6.

FOUCAULT, M. (1977) Discipline and Punish (A. Sheridan, trans.) New York: Random House.

FOX, VERNON (1959) Violence Behind Bars. New York: Vantage Press.

FRIED, CHARLES (1968) "Privacy." Yale Law Journal 77: 475-493.

GABLE, PETER K. (1986) "Application of personal telemonitoring to current problems in corrections." Journal of Criminal Justice 14: 173-182.

GALVIN, JOHN C., WALTER BUSHER, WILLIAM GREENE, GARY KEMP, NORA HARLOW, and KATHLEEN HOFFMAN (1977) Instead of Jail: Pre- and Post-Trial Alternatives to Jail Incarceration, Vol. 4: Sentencing the Misdemeanant. Washington, DC: Government Printing Office.

GARCIA, LT. EUGENE D. (1986) "In-house work release program." Palm Beach County Sheriff's Office, Stockade Division. (mimeo)

GAVISON, RUTH (1980) "Privacy and the limits of law." Yale Law Journal 89: 1577-1622.

GERETY, PIERCE (1980) "A French program to reduce pretrial detention." Crime and Delinquency 26: 22-34.

GETTINGER, STEPHEN (1983) "Intensive supervision, can it rehabilitate probation?" Corrections Magazine 9: 7-18.

GIBBON, EDWARD (1776) The Decline and Fall of the Roman Empire (2nd ed.). London: Strahan.

GIBBONS, DON C. (1982) Society, Crime and Criminal Behavior. Englewood Cliffs, NJ: Prentice-Hall.

GILLIN, JOHN LEWIS (1935) Criminology and Penology. New York: Appleton-Century.

GLASSER, IRA (1974) "Prisoners of benevolence: Power versus liberty in the welfare state," in W. Gaylin et al. (eds.) Doing Good: The Limits of Benevolence. New York: Pantheon.

GOLDSMITH, M. (1983) "The Supreme Court and Title III: Rewriting the law of electronic surveillance." Journal of Criminal Law and Criminology 74: 1-171.

GRAY, FRANCIS C. (1848) Prison Discipline in America. London: John Murray.

GREENBERG, DAVID F. (1975) "Problems in community corrections." Issues in Criminology 7: 1-10.

HAAS, KENNETH C. and JAMES A. INCIARDI (1980) "The Supreme Court and the American crime control effort." Journal of Crime and Justice 3: 141-163.

HALE, MATTHEW (1773) The History of the Pleas of the Crown (1736) (7th ed.). London: Tobey.

HAY, DOUGLAS, PETER LINEBAUGH, JOHN G. RABE, E. P. THOMPSON, and COL. WINSLOW (1975) Albion's Fatal Tree. New York: Pantheon.

HAYLTON, J. H. (1982) "Rhetoric and reality: A critical appraisal of community correctional programs." Crime and Delinquency 28: 314-373.

HONORE, TONY (1978) Tribonion. Ithaca: Cornell University Press.

HUFF, C. RONALD (1980) Field notes (interview in a rural jail), July.

HUFF, C. RONALD (1986) "Home detention as a policy alternative for Ohio's juvenile courts: A final report to the governor's office of criminal justice services." (unpublished)

INCIARDI, JAMES A. (1984) Criminal Justice. Orlando, FL: Academic Press.

Institute for Judicial Administration/American Bar Association (1980) Standards Relating to Interim Statues: The Release, Control, and Detention of Accused Juvenile Offenders between Arrest and Disposition. Cambridge, MA: Ballinger.

Jefferson County, Kentucky, Juvenile Probation Services (1983) Policy and Procedures Manual, Sections 803.11 and 803.12.

JOHNSON, ELMER, H. (1978) Crime, Correction and Society. Homewood, IL: Dorsey.

Kentucky Enquirer (1984) "Kentucky senate given home incarceration bill." January 7: D-1.

Kentucky Enquirer (1985) "Fiscal court eyeing electronic 'jailer.'" January 16: A-1.

Kentucky Post (1984a) "Electronic wardens could reduce jail overcrowding." December 27: 1.

Kentucky Post (1984b) "Home incarceration bill stalled." March 10: 10K.

Kentucky Post (1984c) "Let'm try a small dose." February 15: 4K.

Kentucky Post (1985) "Technology worth trying." January 3: 4K.

KEVE, PAUL C. and CASIMIR S. ZANICK (1972) Final Report and Evaluation of the Home Detention Program, St. Louis, Missouri, September 30 (1971) to July 1 (1972). McLean, VA: Research Analysis Corp.

KRAJICK, KEVIN (1985) Home detention in the computer age. Corrections Compendium 10: 6-9.

LAMBARD, WILLIAM (1581) Eirenarcha or of The Office of the Justices of the Peace. London: Ra. Newbery and H. Bynneman.

LANGAN, PATRICK A. (1985) The Prevalence of Imprisonment. Bureau of Justice Statistics, U.S. Deparment of Justice.

Legislative Record (1985) Is Big Brother Watching? Frankfort: Kentucky General Assembly.

LATHAM, ROBERT and WILLIAM MATTHEWS (1971) The Diary of Samuel Pepys. London: G. Bell.

LERMAN, PAUL (1980) "Trends and Issues in the Deinstitutionalization of Youths in Trouble." Crime and Delinquency 26: 281-298.

LEVIN, H. A. and F. ASKIN (1977) "Privacy in the courts: Law and social reality." Journal of Social Issues 33: 138-153.

LILLY, J. ROBERT (1985) Proposal For: Evaluating Home Incarceration in Kenton County, Kentucky. Submitted to Kentucky Department of Corrections.

LILLY, J. ROBERT and RICHARD A. BALL (1987) "A Brief History of House Arrest and Electronic Monitoring." Northern Kentucky Law Review 13: 343-374.

LILLY, J. ROBERT, RICHARD A. BALL, and JENNIFER WRIGHT (1987) "Home Incarceration and electronic monitoring in Kenton County, Kentucky: An evaluation," in Brenda McCarthy (ed.) Intermediate Punishments: Intensive Supervision and Electronic Surveillance. Monsey, NY: Willowtree.

LILLY, J. ROBERT, RICHARD A. BALL, and W. ROBERT LOTZ, Jr. (1986) "Electronic jails revisited." Justice Quarterly 3: 353-361.

LOFLAND, LYNN (1973) A World of Strangers. New York: Basic Books.

MARX, GARY (1981) "Ironies of social control: Authorities as contributors to deviance through escalation, nonenforcement and covert facilitation." Social Problems 28: 221-246.

McLUHAN, MARSHALL (1965) Understanding Media. New York: McGraw-Hill.

MILLER, ARTHUR P. (1971) The Assault on Privacy. Ann Arbor: University of Michigan Press.

MITFORD, JESSICA (1974) Kind and Usual Punishment. New York: Vantage.

National Advisory Commission on Standards and Goals for Corrections (1973) Report of the National Advisory Commission on Standards and Goals for Corrections. Washington, DC: Government Printing Office.

National Advisory Commission on Standards and Goals for Courts (1973) Report of the National Advisory Commission on Standards and Goals for Courts. Washington, DC: Government Printing Office.

National Advisory Commission on Standards and Goals for the Criminal Justice System (1973) Report of the National Advisory Commission on Standards and Goals for the Criminal Justice System. Washington, DC: Government Printing Office.

National Advisory Committee for Juvenile Justice and Delinquency Prevention (1980) Standards for the Administration of Juvenile Justice. Washington, DC: Government Printing Office.

New York Times (1983) "Jail moves into probationer's home." February 15: 6.

New York Times (1985) "Electronic monitor turns home into jail." February 12: 7.

New York Times (1986) "Fighting narcotics is everyone's issue now." August 10: 25.

Newsweek (1986) "Trying to say 'no.'" August 11: 14-19.

NIEDERBERGER, W. (1984) "Can science save us, revisited." Presented at the annual meeting of the American Society of Criminology.

NIEDERBERGER, W. V. and W. F. WAGNER (1985) Electronic Monitoring of Convicted Offenders: A Field Test. Report to the National Institute of Justice.

Office of Technology Assessment (1985) Electronic surveillance and civil liberties. Washington, DC: Government Printing Office.

Ohio Revised Code (1984) Section 2151. 312.

PACKER, HERBERT (1968) The Limits of Criminal Sanction. Stanford, CA: Stanford University Press.

People (1985) "Tom Moody's electronic cuff keeps tabs on lawbreakers doing time in their own home." October 28: 135.

PETERSILIA, JOAN (1986) "Exploring the option of house arrest." Federal Probation 50: 50-55.

POLLOCK, FREDRICH and FREDRICK W. MAITLAND (1968) The History of English Law, Vol. II. London: Cambridge University Press.

President's Commission on Law Enforcement and Administration of Justice (1967) The Challenge of Crime in a Free Society. Washington, DC: Government Printing Office.

PROSSER, WILLIAM (1960) "Privacy." California Law Review 48: 383-423.

REIMAN, JEFFREY (1976) "Privacy, intimacy and personhood." Philosophy and Public Affairs 6(1): 26-44.

RUBIN, H. TED (1985) Juvenile justice: Policy, Practice, and Law (2nd ed.). New York: Random House.

RUBIN, H. TED (1979) Juvenile justice: Policy, Practice, and Law. Santa Monica, CA: Goodyear.

RUSCHE, GEORGE and OTTO KIRCHHEIMER (1968) Punishment and Social Structure. New York: Russell and Russell.

RUSCHE, GEORGE (1933) "Labor market and penal sanction: Thoughts on the sociology of criminal justice." In Tony Platt and Paul Takagi (eds.) Punishment and Penal Discipline (1980). San Francisco: Crime and Social Justice Association.

RUTHERFORD, ANDREW and OSMAN BENGUR (1976) Community-Based Alternatives to Juvenile Incarceration. Washington, DC: National Institute of Law Enforcement and Criminal Justice.

San Diego County, California Probation Department (1986) Personal correspondence (February).

SCHMIDT, ANNESLEY K. (1986) "Electronic monitoring." Federal Probation 50: 56-59.

SCHWARTZ, HERMAN (1977) Taps, Bugs, and Fooling the People. New York: Field Foundation.

SCOTT, SAMUEL P. [ed.] (1932) Corpus Juris Civilis: The Civil Law. Cincinnati: Central Trust Co.

SELLIN, THORSTEN J. (1944) Pioneering in Penology. New York: Elsevier.

SELLIN, THORSTEN J. (1970) "The origin of the 'Pennsylvania system of prison discipline.'" Prison Journal 2: 12-22.

Semayne's Case (1604) 5 Coke's Reports 91.

SENNA, J. J. and L. J. SIEGEL (1984) Introduction to Criminal Justice (3rd ed.). St. Paul, MN: West.

SHANK, GREGORY (1980) "Thorsten Sellin's peneology," in Tony Platt and Paul Takagi (eds.) Punishment and Penal Discipline (1980). San Francisco: Crime and Social Justice Association.

SHORTER, EDWARD (1977) The Making of the Modern Family. New York: Basic Books.

SMITH, JOAN and WILLIAM FRIED (1975) The Uses of the American Prison. Lexington, MA: Lexington.

SMYKA, J. and W. C. SELKE (1982) "The impact of home detention: A less restrictive alternative to the detention of juveniles." Juvenile and Family Court Journal (May): 3-9.

SUTHERLAND, EDWIN H. and DONALD R. CRESSEY (1978) Criminology. Philadelphia: Lippincott.

SWANK, WILLIAM G. (1979) "Home supervision: Probation really works." Federal Probation (December): 50-52.

TAFT, DONALD R. and RALPH W. ENGLAND, Jr. (1964) Criminology. New York: Macmillan.

TAKAGI, PAUL (1975) "The Walnut Street jail: A penal reform to centralize the powers of the state." Federal Probation 39: 18-26.

TANNENBAUM, FRANK (1938) Crime and Community. Boston: Ginn.

The Economist (1985) "Electronic beacons: Four walls do not a prison make." March 30: 90-92.

Time (1985) "Spiderman's net: An electronic alternative to prison." October 14: 34.

Time (1986) "Crack down: Reagan declares war on drugs and proposes tests for key officials." August 18: 12-13.

TURNER, J. W. CECIL (1966) Kenny's Outline of Criminal Law (9th ed.). Cambridge: Cambridge University Press.

20/20 (1986) "Prisoners in Their Own Homes." American Broadcasting Corporation.

VINTER, ROBERT D., THEODORE M. NEWCOMB, and RHEA KISH [eds.] (1976) Time Out: A National Study of Juvenile Correctional Programs. Ann Arbor: University of Michigan Press.

Wall Street Journal (1986) "Monitors permit house arrest instead of jail." March 17: 19.

WARREN, SAMUEL D. and LOUIS D. BRANDEIS (1890) "The right to privacy." Harvard Law Review 4: 192-220.

Washington Post (1985) "Va. looks to in-house to keep offenders on line, in line." November 2: A 22.

Washington Post (1986) "Drug tests called costly, often useless." June 21: 6-15.

WATSON, ALAN [trans. and ed.] (1985) The Digest of Justinian. Philadelphia: University of Pennsylvania Press.

WEINBERG, KENNETH G. (1971) A Man's Home, A Man's Castle. New York: McCall.

WESTIN, ALAN F. (1967) Privacy and Freedom. New York: Atheneum.

WOLFE, MAXINE and ROBERT S. LAUFER (1974) "The concept of privacy in childhood and adolescence," in D. H. Carson (ed.) Main-Environment Interactions: Evaluations and Applications. Washington, DC: Environmental Design Research Association.

YOUNG, THOMAS M. and DONNELL M. PAPPENFORT (1977) Secure detention of juveniles and alternatives to its use. National Evaluation Program, Summary Report, Phase I. National Institute of Law Enforcement and Criminal Justice, LFAA. Washington, DC: Government Printing Office.

CASES

Bearden v. Georgia 1983. 461 U.S. 660.
Bell v. Wolfish, 1979. 441 U.S. 520.
Berger v. New York 1967. 388 U.S. 41.

Bowers v. Hardwick 1986. 106 S.Ct. 2841.

Brady v. United States 1971. 397 U.S. 742.

Carchedi v. Rhodes 1982. 560 F. Supp. 1010 (S.D. Ohio).

Edwards v. California 1941. 314 U.S. 160.

Ettore v. Philco Television Broadcasting Company 1956. 229 F. 2d. 481 (3rd Cir.).

Gagnon v. Scarpelli 1973. 411 U.S. 778.

Goergen v. State 1959. 18 Misc. 2d 1085, 196 N.Y.S. 2d 455 (Ct. Cl.).

Goldman v. United States 1942. 316 U.S. 129.

Graham v. Richardson 1971. 403 U.S. 365.

Greco v. Georgia 1976. 429 U.S. 1301.

Greenholtz v. Nebraska Penal Inmates 1979. 442 U.S. 1.

Griswold v. Connecticut 1965. 381 U.S. 298.

Higdon v. United States 1980. 627 F2d 893 (9th Cir.).

Hoffa v. Saxbe 1974. 378 F. Suppl. 1221 (D.D.C.).

Hudson v. Palmer 1984. 468 U.S. 517.

Hyland v. Procunier 1970. 311 F. Supp. 749 (N.D. Cal.).

Irvine v. California 1954. 347 U.S. 128, 74 S.Ct. 381.

Johnson v. State 1968. 69 Cal. 2d 782, 447 P 2d 352, 73 Cal. Rptr. 240.

Katz v. United States 1967. 389 U.S. 347.

Latta v. Fitzharris 1975. 521 F2d. 246 (9th Cir).

Mapp v. Ohio 1961. 367 U.S. 643, 81 S.Ct. 1684.

Minnesota v. Murphy 1984. 465 U.S. 420.

Morrisey v. Brewer 1972. 408 U.S. 471.

Meyers v. Los Angeles County Probation Department 1978. 78 Cal. App. 3d 309, 144
    Cal. Rptr. 186.

NAACP v. Alabama 1958. 357 U.S. 449, 78 S.Ct. 1243.

Olmstead v. United States 1928. 227 U.S. 438.

Panko v. McCauley 1979. 473 F. Suppl. 325 (E.D. Wisc).

People v. Mason 1971. S Cal. 3d 759, 488 P. 2d 630, 97 Cal. Rptr. 302.

People v. Morgan 1982. 206 Neb. 818, 295 N. W. 2d 285.

Porth v. Templar 1971. 453 F2d. 330 (10th Cir.).

Rakas v. Illinois. 1978. 439 U.S. 128.

Reiser v. District of Columbia 1977. 563 F. 2d 462 (D.C. Cir.).

Roe v. Wade 1973. 410 U.S. 113.

Schall v. Martin 1984. 467 U.S. 253, 104 S.Ct. 2403.

Schuemann v. Colorado State Board of Adult Parole 1980. 624 F2d 172 (10th Cir.).

Silverman v. United States 1961. 365 U.S. 505.

Smith v. Maryland 1979. 442 U.S. 735.

Sobell v. Reed 1971 327 F. Supp. 1294 (S.D.N.Y.)

State v. Bollinger 1971. 169 N.J. Super 553, 405 A. 2d 432.

State v. Cooper 1981. 282 S. E. 2d 436 (N.C.).

State v. Earnest 1980. 293 N. W. 2d. 365 (Minn.).

State v. Gallagher 1984. 100 N. M. 697, 675 P. 2d 429 (N.M. App.)

State v. Montgomery 1977. 115 Ariz. 583, 566 P. 2d 1329.

State v. Sprague 1981. 52 Or. App. 1063, 629 P. 2d 1326 (Or. Ct. App.).

Sweeny v. United States 1965. 353 F.2d 10 (7th Cir.).

Tinker v. Des Moines School District 1969. 393 U.S. 503.

Trop v. Dulles 1958. 356 U.S. 86.

United States ex rel Coleman v. Smith 1975, 395 F. Supp. 1155 (W.D.N.Y.)

United States ex rel Santos v. New York Board of Parole 1971. 441 F2d. 1216 (2d Cir.).

United States v. Bradley 1978. 571 F.2d 787 (4th Cir.).

United States v. Bruneau 1979. 594 F2d 1190 (8th Cir.).

United States v. Consuelo-Gonzalez 1975. 521 F. 2d 259 (9th Cir.)

United States v. Furukawa 1979. 596 F. 2d 921 (9th Cir.).

United States v. Jiminez 1980. 600 F. 2d 1152 (5th Cir.).

United States v. Karo 1984. 468 U.S. 705.

United States v. Knotts 1983. 460 U.S. 276.

United States v. Miroyan 1978. 577 F. 2d 489 (9th Cir.).

United States v. Mitsubishi International Corporation 1982. 677 F. 2d. 785 (9th Cir.).

United States v. New York Telephone Company 1977. 434 U.S. 159.

United States v. Scott 1982. 678 F. 2d 32 (5th Cir.).

United States v. Thomas 1984. 729 F. 2d 120 (2d Cir.).

United States v. Tonry 1979. 605 F. 2d 144 (5th Cir.).

United States v. White 1971. 401 U.S. 745.

United States v. Workman 1978. 585 F. 2d 1205 (4th Cir.).

Utah v. Valasquez 1983. 672 P. 2d 1254.

About the Authors

Richard A. Ball is Professor of Sociology at West Virginia University. He received his B.A. from West Virginia University in 1958, his M.A. from that institution in 1960, and his Ph.D. from Ohio State University in 1965. He has authored several monographs and approximately 100 articles and book chapters, including articles in the *American Journal of Corrections, American Sociological Review, The American Sociologist, British Journal of Social Psychiatry, Crime and Delinquency, Criminology, Federal Probation, International Journal of Comparative and Applied Criminal Justice, International Social Science Review, Journal of Communication, Journal of Small Business Management, Journal of Psychohistory, Justice Quarterly, Northern Kentucky Law Review, Qualitative Sociology, Rural Sociology, Social Forces, Social Problems, Sociological Focus, Sociological Symposium, Sociology and Social Welfare, Sociology of Work and Occupations, Urban Life, Victimology,* and *World Futures.* His research in interests include home incarceration, criminological theory, social problems theory, sociology of law, and women inmates. He is coauthor of *American Criminological Theory: Its Context and Consequences* with Sage Publications (forthcoming).

C. Ronald Huff is Professor of Public Administration and Director of Ohio State University's Criminal Justice Research Center. He previously served on the faculties of the University of California (Irvine) and Purdue University. His previous publications include five books and more than thirty papers in scholarly journals or edited volumes. He is currently completing a sixth book, *Convicted but Innocent: Wrongful Conviction and Public Policy* (Ohio State University Press), which is coauthored by Arye Rattner and the late Edward Sagarin.

J. Robert Lilly is Professor of Criminology and Adjunct Professor of Law at Northern Kentucky University. His research interests include juvenile delinquency, house arrest and electronic monitoring, criminal justice in the People's Republic of China, the sociology of law, and criminological theory. He has published in *Criminology, Crime and Delinquency, Social Problems, Legal Studies Forum, Northern Kentucky Law Review, Journal of Drug Issues, The New Scholar, Adolescence, Qualitative Sociology, Federal Probation, International Journal of Comparative and Applied Criminal Justice,* and *Justice Quarterly.* He has coauthored several articles and book chapters with Richard A. Ball, and he is coauthor of *American Criminological Theory: Its Context and Consequences* with Sage Publications (forthcoming). He is also the Treasurer of the American Society of Criminology.

NOTES

NOTES

NOTES

NOTES